Third Base Is My Home

PHOTO BY FRED KEENAN
The Patriot Ledger

Third Base Is My Home

Brooks Robinson

As told to JACK TOBIN

WORD BOOKS, Publisher
Waco, Texas

To those dearest to me—
my wife, Connie,
our children, Brooks David, Chris, Michael,
and Diana,
and my parents
all of whom have shared in the hours of success
and the hours of sorrow

Preface

Many writers and broadcasters have painted majestic portraits of my abilities as a baseball player. Now I've strayed into their field to try and give my own insights into a career that has realized all my boyhood dreams.

Not only would it be impossible to recite every detail of every event of that career, it would make a boring book. So instead, I've made stops along my years to try and point up those events—large and small—that seem important to me. It is difficult to be sure you've chosen wisely, and even when the choices have been made, it's not always possible to treat them with equal care.

Every person I've encountered has in his own way left an imprint on my life, and every player I've been associated with, from sandlot to Series games, has helped me along. I wish I could thank them all personally . . . those who have taught me, from my parents and my schoolteachers on through to the managers and coaches who have so painstakingly shared their knowledge of the game I love . . . and those who have assisted me over the years—trainers, clubhouse men, secretaries, fellow players, business associates, and personal friends. No one does it alone.

Writing this book is not an attempt on my part to enter a new field. Rather, by telling my story I have tried to accomplish two things that are very important to me. I hope I have expressed my deep appreciation for the little things that make life so rewarding in such a way that readers may find a new awareness of those feelings in their own experience. Then I would like to think that, for my young readers especially, at least some portions of my life story—the problems as well as the successes—may be enough like their own to be of help and guidance.

If even a part of this happens, my mission here may some day go down in the record books as a success.

BROOKS ROBINSON

Lutherville, Maryland
April 1974

1

The weatherman must have heard our complaints, because Friday morning was bright and clear and almost
warm. Quite a contrast to the chilly day before when we'd
have done better throwing snowballs than baseballs and
wearing stocking caps instead of baseball helmets. The
hint of green in the grass didn't do much to hide the fact
that the ground was rock hard, especially the new bumps
in the infield where it had been redone after the close of
the Baltimore Colts' football season.

The thermometer was in the mid-fifties and slowly
creeping up when I went out on the field. The grounds crew
was still doing some last-minute finishing up. The stands
were empty except for concession men stocking their booths
and other personnel hanging the flags.

I'd left my home in Lutherville about ten that morning

for the ten-mile drive on the Beltway to Memorial Stadium. The exhilarating anticipation of the opening day game was familiar, but I realized all over again, too, how much I love the game of baseball. There's never been a day—even when things weren't going well—that it's been a drag for me to play. Whether it's just a workout, a league game, or a day with special meaning that makes the adrenalin flow a little faster—like this one—I look forward to getting to the park. And, whatever the circumstances, being ready mentally is number one in my book. That means being there in plenty of time.

Throughout spring training I'd been working intensively with Jimmy Frey, our hitting coach, trying to get my reflexes pin sharp. Today I took more than my share of batting practice, concentrating very closely to avoid bringing my arms into my body—a fault Jimmy had me working to overcome. But I wasn't pleased with what was happening. While I was making fair contact with the ball, it wasn't zinging off the bat the way I wanted it to, any more than it had the last few weeks or last season either, for that matter.

I sure didn't like what had happened to my batting average last season. Between 1971 and 1972 it had dropped twenty-two points. And it was disturbing to go down from ninety-two to sixty-four runs batted in, but what really shook me was to get only eight homers when I'd had twenty the year before. To add insult to injury, I'd even had a fielding slump early in 1972—seven errors in the first thirty games. Fortunately, from then on I had only four more in the entire season.

After all, I was thirty-five. Was I really going to have to start admitting, "This is it—the way down"?

When batting practice was over, I checked the field once more and then headed for the clubhouse, still preoccupied with my hitting. The thrill of opening day excitement was unmistakably in the air as I went "rag-picking" for a bat— something I often do before a game. (Ask anyone who knows me—I've even borrowed from players on visiting clubs.) But nothing in our stock seemed to feel just right, or anything in the "dead bat" bin where we toss our discards. Finally, after I'd circled the clubhouse a time or two, I asked Enos Cabell, a rookie infielder, if I could borrow one of his sticks, a deep brown-toned bat. It felt better than anything else, certainly better than any in my own collection.

At least I didn't have the worry of not being in shape. I'd worked hard in the off-season and in Florida too. My legs were good and my arm wasn't hurting; in fact, I felt sure that I could cover as much ground and get at any ball as well as when I joined the Orioles seventeen years ago.

Statistics say our crowd this 1973 opening day was only 26,543. Still, that was about 25,000 more than we'd averaged for our Florida exhibition games, and enough people in the stands to give you that special tingly feeling up and down your spine.

When the manager, Earl Weaver, posted the batting order, I was hitting sixth. That's at least three spots higher than I should have been, based on what I had done with my bat in Florida.

Milwaukee was starting a young right-hander from California named Jim Colborn. He hadn't pitched enough in the American League by then for anyone really to know much about him. We got to him real quick in the first inning.

Suddenly the public address announcer was calling out: "Now batting . . . Brooks Robinson . . . third base."

There I was with Cabell's bat, two men on base, and a batting average that wasn't too far away from my weight —and you never boast about 195 unless you're advertising how trim you are.

Colborn's first pitch came down just a bit outside, about waist high—the kind I like. It resembled nothing so much as a big balloon as I swung at it. Once that brown bomber met the ball, there was no doubt that it was gone. It was no tape-measure job, but I was mighty satisfied as I ran toward first watching it carry into the fourth or fifth row of the left field bleachers.

Perhaps this was an omen of things to come, I remember thinking as I tagged third and could hear the cheers and calls from the guys on the bench over the noise of the crowd. That ball was about as well hit as any I had connected with all spring.

The first person I looked for in the dugout was Enos. I wanted to tell him thank you.

It wasn't until much later, when I looked back over the stats, that I suddenly realized I hadn't hit my first home run in 1972 until June 6, my 146th time at bat. And then when I got another in the eighth inning off Bill Champion, this turned out to be as good an opening day as I'd had in many years.

On that second homer, as I rounded third base I told the umpire, Joe Brinkman, that I hadn't hit two homers in a game since 1956 when I was with San Antonio in the Texas League. Later, however, I remembered hitting two in a single game more recently than that here at Memorial Stadium off Joe Horlen of the White Sox.

And in the clubhouse after the game when I was talking

with the sports writers, we recalled four or five other opening days when I hit solo homers and also that I had gone four for four in Baltimore in the 1958 opener. Big days like this are always a thrill, but they seem more important now, probably because all the writers and broadcasters keep reminding me that I'm not that eighteen-year-old kid just up from Little Rock.

I've seen a lot of players "hang 'em up," not because they are physically tired but because they're mentally worn out. I'm not mentally tired at all. I look forward to the challenge of coming out for this great game every day. My wife, Connie, keeps me pumped up. She thinks I'm going to play forever.

And you know something? I wouldn't mind that at all.

Chapter 2

It's a pretty sure thing that the player's bat is what speaks loudest when it's contract time, but there are moments when the glove has the last word.

Sportswriters and fans too are always asking, "What's the greatest moment you've had in baseball?" That question is always difficult to answer, but on a scale of 1 to 10, the 1970 World Series between our Baltimore Orioles and the Cincinnati Reds would be pushing for number one with me. We eliminated the Cincinnati Reds in five games, I was named the Most Valuable Player, and, most important, it erased the humiliation of our defeat in 1969 by the New York Mets.

In the ninth inning of that fifth game, with two men gone, Pat Corrales, batting for Hal McRae, rapped a ground ball straight to me. Scooping it up, I pegged it over to first, and when it popped in Boog Powell's glove on first base for the last out, that was it. We were World Champions, and it was my putout that had clinched it.

Thinking back on it later, I realized the first time any hint of being named Most Valuable Player penetrated my thoughts was in our half of the eighth inning. With Frank Robinson on second and Merv Rettenmund on first, I was called out on strikes. As I walked away from the plate shaking my head and talking to myself, suddenly it dawned on me that those people standing up in the stands cheering and clapping were making all that noise for me.

But those thoughts were almost instantly blotted out in our half of the ninth inning. Johnny Bench, leading off for the Reds, hit a scorching shot down the line. I dove instinctively toward third and the ball ripped into my glove for an out. When Lee May struck out and Corrales grounded out, that ended it all and the ecstasy of a championship was ours.

To read some of the writeups the next day, you'd have thought that Brooks Robinson had done it all alone. Everyone agreed I deserved the MVP award, but from my point of view twenty-five guys had won that title. It was fine to have the car that was the award for being named MVP, but I wish the rest of them could have had one too.

Every World Series winners' clubhouse inevitably is marked by bedlam, and that was certainly true of ours. A moment that I'll always appreciate took place after a bit of calm had begun to reappear. Ken Smith, the director of the Baseball Hall of Fame in Cooperstown, New York, asked me for the glove I had used in the series.

Now that is a high honor. Ken reminded me that one of the gloves in the hall, for example, belonged to Joe (Ducky) Medwick, the famous outfielder of the St. Louis Cardinals.

We used to hear their games in Little Rock, and I can remember how impressed I was with the great plays he made.

Ken mentioned that the Hall also had enshrined one of the bats used by Pie Traynor, the greatest third baseman of all time. He pointed out that people keep comparing me to Traynor. That's a great honor, I know, because the old-timers I've talked with tell some fantastic tales about Traynor's feats with both the glove and the bat.

Ken had already spoken to me about getting the glove after the third game of the series, as a matter of fact, a day that had been one of the greatest of my life. I took two legitimate hits away from Johnny Bench as we won, 9–3, primarily due to the first grand slam home run ever hit by a pitcher, Dave McNally, who was on the mound for us in that game.

When Ken asked me for my glove and Dave for his bat, of course we both said yes. But I soon regretted having so readily agreed to give it up. Gloves are almost a fetish with me. I'm always searching for one that feels right. When you need a new one it's a lot bigger problem than finding a new bat, even though bats break often and gloves only get too loose when you've used them a few years.

After agreeing to give the series glove to Ken, I tried during the whole off season to come up with another, but there just didn't seem to be a single one that was made for me. Finally I had to ask Ken if I could keep the glove for 1971, or at least until I found a new glove. I used it the entire season, not shipping it to Cooperstown until after we'd lost to Pittsburgh in a tight seven-game series.

That glove wasn't really mine anyway. It came from Dave May, a former outfielder for us. I was wandering around the clubhouse one day testing the feel of extra gloves that various players had in their bins when I came upon this one of Dave's. It seemed to have what I wanted

[16]

in the leather and in the way it was molded. But it was the way it felt on my hand that counted most, so I made a deal with Dave—two of my gloves for his one. It was the best glove swap ever for me. Dave, who was traded to Milwaukee early in that 1970 season, needled me about that glove all the time, especially when they showed a TV commercial I made with it. You could see Dave's name scratched out on the leather and mine written in with a black marking pen.

I may be the biggest glove hound in baseball. I've traded for gloves with a lot of players over the years—Dick Bosman, a pitcher with the Cleveland Indians; Curt Motton, who played outfield for us; Tommy Davis, with the Dodgers when we played in our first series; Jerry DeVanon, a member of our team before going to the Angels; Donnie Baylor, our young outfielder. And there have been many others. Almost every glove cost me a two-for-one trade, like the series glove that was Dave May's and the game glove I'm using now.

Regardless of where a player finds his glove, it's absolutely essential to get it in shape. Once I find one I want—and that usually means trying ten to fifteen different gloves—it takes me about a year to get it ready. I don't soak it in water, wrap it around a ball with rubber bands, or anything like that.

The first thing I do is tighten up the lacing to my needs. Then I usually take a little padding out by the side of the thumb and down by the heel, at the base of the palm. This makes the pocket in the glove flatter. A hard heel with a large rise seems to make the ball bounce away further, sometimes for an error, while the flat pocket gives you a better chance the ball will stick in it. And then all I do to break the glove in is to use it in practice.

When I've chosen a game glove, I use it for three or four

[17]

years, depending on how long it stays firm. And I never use my game glove except for game play. I have a second glove to use when I field batting practice, and another for infield workouts. Usually the infield glove is one I'm breaking in to replace my game glove.

What kind of glove do I like? A real soft glove never works with me, nor a real stiff one. It's got to be somewhere in between—not too firm, not too limber, something that just feels right. And once you've found it, you can't be too careful how you treat it.

From what I've observed over the years, it seems that I'm more protective of my glove than most players. I'm especially careful when we travel. We're responsible for packing our own gear, and I always make sure my glove is wrapped well in my uniform before stowing it in my road bag. I don't want it getting caught on my spikes or getting hurt as the bags are thrown at the airports and in the cargo areas of our planes. And I take great pains to see that it's not lost or stolen.

My glove has always been my trademark, and many fans have commended me on my fielding in the years since the 1970 series. It really makes you feel good to know that they remember those plays and that they'll go out of their way to tell you about it.

Having my 1970 series glove go to the Hall of Fame meant a lot to me. But the next year when it was contract time, Harry Dalton, then our general manager, put a lot more weight to my other World Series statistics—.429 batting average, two home runs, and six runs batted in—than to my .958 fielding average in the 1970 series.

With so much emphasis on hitting, probably more players try to keep track of the particular bat they've taken a liking to than the glove they use in the field. But I'm as dependent on my game glove as Kenny Getler, a fellow I used to play against in the Texas League, was on his glasses. That was back in my San Antonio days. At the time, Kenny was the leading home run hitter in the Texas League even though he wore that big thick bottle kind of glasses.

One night Kenny's glasses disappeared. When he had to sit out two or three games waiting for a new pair to come from home, it made me wonder what kind of shape I'd be in if I ever lost my glove. It would be mighty tough to go out there at third some night with a glove that wasn't ready.

That's when you realize how important that crazy-shaped piece of leather is to your career in the major leagues.

Chapter 3

As far back as I can remember, I had baseball on my mind. Mother and Dad tell me the first words I ever really learned were "Play ball, Daddy," and they've got a picture of me when I was seventeen months old with a ball cap on and a baseball clutched in both hands.

I came by my passion for baseball quite naturally. Dad played a lot of semipro ball and an even greater amount of softball at night. In fact, the year I was born he played for the World Softball Championship on an International Harvester team out of Little Rock. They went to the finals at Soldier Field in Chicago but lost to a team from Cincinnati, 2–1. Baseball was his best game, though, and there's not the slightest doubt his love for it rubbed off on me.

If ever a father helped a son make the major leagues, mine helped me. I was hardly big enough to hold a glove up when he taught me to catch a rubber baseball. And one of my earliest memories is the day he cut off an old broom so the handle was about the right size for me to swing like a bat. At first all I did was hit that rubber baseball back to him, but as I got a little bigger, I discovered the back alley and the rocks. It was a kid's dream.

We were living at 2012 Lloyd Court at the time, and rolling down from the alley was a series of little knolls that finally flattened out into a sort of grass meadow with a stand of small trees at its edge. Other kids called them the woods, but to me they were left, center, and right fields. That's where I took batting practice.

There were thousands and thousands of rocks on the unpaved road behind our house, and there's no telling how many of them I hit into the meadow—and once in a while over "the fence," as I called the woods. From the time I was big enough to swing my broomstick bat, I was out there every chance I could get.

Mom and the neighbors could always tell where I was by the ping of the rocks against those old broomsticks. I was probably seven or eight when I really became proficient with one. From then on I scoured the neighborhood begging worn-out brooms from every house around. I must have gone through a hundred or so during those years on Lloyd Court.

We lived there until my last year in junior high when I was about fifteen. By then I could wallop a rock a good long way. I found out just how far one afternoon when in my imagination I was playing with the Cardinals in old Sportsman's Park. I really laid into one good-sized rock, and suddenly I heard this screaming "Kaw!" That rock I'd figured for a homer over the "right field fence" had hit a big black crow on the wing.

I didn't even know he was flying by, but when the rock hit him, he fluttered down crazily toward the woods like a falling plane. I ran to the spot where I thought he'd landed and after a few minutes found him lying on the ground, stunned and bleeding a little. Carefully picking him up, I hurried home with him and tried to describe to Mom what had happened. We kept him around a few days nursing him back to health. One day he just flapped his wings and took off.

Though the experience scared me when it took place, I really enjoyed the notoriety it brought me. Most of the kids on the block knew about it almost as quick as the crow did, and they all came over to see the victim. By the end of the next day in school everyone in West Little Rock had heard the story from friends, of course with the facts embellished considerably.

To this day a game of pepper takes me back to those afternoons in the alley along Lloyd Court. We had various versions of baseball then. If we didn't have enough for nine on a side we'd play short. If we were too short, we'd play scrub, knock up, and lay down, and six grounders and three flies—anything to hit and catch a ball. And if there were just two or three, we'd play pepper. Every once in a while when we're playing an exhibition somewhere or when we're down in Florida in spring training, I'll catch myself picking up a stray pebble from the playing field and socking it out with a bat. I guess we never really outgrow our childhood.

But if I wasn't batting rocks in the alley, I'd be out throwing a tennis ball against the steps in front of the house. There were sixteen of those steps, and the ball would hop back to me either in the air or as a grounder, depending on where I threw it. If it hit up about halfway, it would sometimes act almost like a pop fly. I wore out nearly as many balls against the steps as I did broomsticks in the alley.

Looking back, I can see I was lucky to have been born in Little Rock and to have lived where we did—across the street from the Arkansas School for the Deaf, a residence school with good practice fields and a nice gym. Also, the whole town, with its tremendous interest in sports, seemed to have more than its share of kids with athletic talent. And we had plenty of inspiration from the Arkansas Travelers of the Southern Association, as well as from the semipro teams that played on Sundays over at Lamar Porter Field.

When I was younger, I used to work on the scoreboard at Lamar Porter Field during semipro games or sell cold drinks. Once in a while I worked on the grandstand shagging fly balls that went up on top. But the big deal was to get to operate the scoreboard. We had to hang the numbers by hand. When you were little that meant getting on your tiptoes to put up a score for the inning.

Interest in softball was running especially high in Little Rock when I was in the early grades, and almost every grammar school had a team. That was where I got my earliest experience on an honest-to-goodness organized ball club. I started out as a catcher for Woodruff School, although later I played mostly in the infield. As a matter of fact, one of the first prizes I ever won was the junior distance softball throw in a 4th of July contest sponsored by the Little Rock Parks and Recreation Department when I was just a little past ten years old.

When I was old enough to go out for Midget League baseball the next year, I was placed on the Franklin Paint Bulldogs, a team known as the "Yankees of the Midget League." I played mostly the same positions I had for

[23]

Woodruff, but did a little pitching too, even racking up a no-hit, no-run game on one occasion when we ran up a 19–0 score against our opponents. For a bunch of little guys we were pretty good, winning the city championship and a year later the state title as well.

Throughout my teen years, much of the time when we weren't practicing or playing a game for one of the league teams or the school, I was over at the Deaf School gym. Actually, I wasn't supposed to be hanging around there. The only legitimate reason I had for that, other than just wanting to play ball—any kind of ball—was that one of my best friends in junior high had an older brother attending the school. We played a lot of basketball. There were some super players there, and their school team won the national and world championships for deaf students a time or two.

I could handle their finger language well enough to get by, thanks to that innate ability you have when you're young for catching on fast to anything new. Every so often even now I'll glance up into the stands and see some fan spell out B-R-O-O-K-S to me. If he goes slowly enough I can still converse a little bit.

But what really mattered most in my growing-up years was the attention Dad gave me. Fortunately, his job as a fireman gave him long blocks of time off as compensation for the twenty-four hour shifts he had to work, and he was never too busy to spend a lot of that time with me. He's the one responsible for my love of baseball and especially my desire to do the best I can every day. He's also the one who instilled in me the ability to forget today's game and prepare for tomorrow, a fundamental requirement in any sport. You've got to correct your mistakes but not dwell on them to the extent that they become more important than what lies ahead.

I'll always be grateful to my dad for having the insight to keep just the right balance between play and practice. He never put any pressure on me, and I never remember him correcting me about how I played in a game unless I asked. If I wanted to field some grounders, he'd drop everything to go out and hit them to me. Then he'd pitch batting practice to me by the hour so I could hit. He never told me, "You've got to do it this way"; it was always, "Why don't you try this?"

I can still remember the moment that I consciously began to appreciate what Dad had been doing for me. It came when we were walking home after one of our impromptu workouts and there was nothing unusual to account for it. I was just suddenly overwhelmed to realize how important a dad like mine is when you're in high school and dreaming of playing in the big leagues.

To this day I can't say enough about Dad's influence on me, both as a man and as an athlete. And my admiration and respect for him continue to grow.

Throwing a paper route is something you do almost automatically, after the first two or three weeks anyway. It's
just like making the second baseman's pivot for the
double-play relay. For me that made it a good place to do
some thinking. And as my ninth-grade graduation loomed
closer, there was a problem important enough to keep my
mind pretty well occupied for the three hours or so it took
me to deliver papers to a hundred and fifty customers.

Mrs. Hillard, one of my eighth-grade teachers, had really
brought it up the year before when she made a major assignment to our English class. We were to write a term
paper on what we thought our professions would be. I
titled mine "Why I Want to Play Professional Baseball."
Somewhere I had found a picture of Ernie Lombardi, which
I used on the cover. Inside were other photographs—a shot

of the Cardinals in a World Series game, a double play with one guy riding another on the throw to first base. That one had a caption I still remember—"The Piggyback Putout."

I wrote all about what life was like for a professional baseball player from the majors down to the D leagues. Somewhere I'd found information on salary levels, but I must have estimated several—especially for the majors—because I recall writing that there was no limit to the money you could make in the big leagues.

The assignment included some specific points. Where we had to list our assets I remember stating, "I am not easily discouraged." And where we were to evaluate or appraise our disposition, my comment was, "I'm slow to anger and not easily discouraged; am enthusiastic, happy, calm, and very active." In addition we had to explain our reasons for selecting that particular profession. I wrote: "The hours are good and ball players are paid very well."

Then I shared my big dream. "If I make the major leagues," I confided, "the one thing I want to do is play for the St. Louis Cardinals. What I like to do best is play third base or pitch. When you pitch you have a better chance to make the majors because baseball teams carry seven or eight pitchers while they carry only two players for each base."

It's obvious that at thirteen I wasn't much of a prophet. If I'd had to stay in the major leagues as a pitcher, I wouldn't have made it.

I probably wouldn't have made it as a football player either, although our ninth-grade football team at Pulaski Heights Junior High, on which I was a regular, compiled an excellent record. That was also the only year I ever played organized football. I had never gone out for it before, and didn't really intend to then. But the team's quarterback had graduated and gone on to high school, and some of the guys—Johnny Crawford, a guard, and Scott Woodmansee, one of my best friends, who played halfback—talked me into it. They felt I was a good passer and could fill the quarterback spot for them.

Our success in the 1951 season wasn't due to Brooks Robinson, quarterback, but to some real good players and our coach, Winston Faulkner. We won nine games and tied one with North Little Rock, 6–6, and then went on to win the state championship by defeating Pine Bluff, 20–0; Hot Springs, 18–8; and El Dorado, 26–0. Four of the players— Woodmansee; Bill Eshelman, an end; Herbie Rule, a tackle; and Ralph Goldman, a halfback—all made first team All-State. Johnny Crawford made second team and fullback Darrell Herbert and I received honorable mention.

That one season in football created a real problem for me, one that consumed a major part of my paper-route thinking time as the year rolled by. Wilson Matthews, the head coach at Little Rock Senior, had made it quite plain that he wanted me to play for him. In fact, he had already made a point of telling me several times that a football scholarship was the best way for an athlete to assure himself of getting a college education.

Knowing how much my parents hoped I would go to college, I was finding it extremely difficult to tell them how I felt. But I had already made up my mind about my future, and, as my eighth-grade paper on my vocation had pointed out, football was not really part of it.

All this came tumbling out one rainy morning when my dad was with me on my paper route. He took me around in the blue Nash occasionally when the papers were particularly big or when the weather was bad. I had just tossed a paper to the house where Bill Dickey used to live —he was the great New York Yankee catcher my dad always talks about—and we were nearly through for one more day. Just what gave me the courage to start such a serious discussion then I don't remember. But when I got back in the car, I decided to confess how I really felt about my future career in sports.

"You know," I began, "I had a pretty good football season, and now it looks like Coach wants me to go out at Little Rock Senior. He tells me it's the best way to get a college athletic scholarship. I know you and Mom want me to go to college, and I don't want to do anything you wouldn't like. But I've made up my mind that I want to play major league baseball. When you play football, you run a risk of getting a busted knee or shoulder. That might ruin my baseball."

Dad was always great at times like that. He turned off the key in the Nash when I started talking and heard me out.

"I know your feeling, Buddy," Dad said, using the nickname he and Mom called me most of the time. "If I had a choice to make, knowing how you always favored baseball, that would be mine too."

As to college, Dad told me that was also for me to decide, that if baseball was more important I could always go to college in the winter or later on.

When we got home for breakfast, we went over my problem again with Mom. She voiced her agreement: "It wouldn't be right for us to try and force you to do something you didn't want to do."

For several mornings after that I thought about my decision as I took care of my route. The more I thought about it, the more right it seemed.

It wasn't long until those donuts and milk I was in the habit of consuming at Grissham's Grocery when I'd finished throwing my papers began to taste better again. So did the real breakfast Mom had ready for me when I got home a few minutes later. And I could be more cheerful on my way to school now that I felt I'd reached the right solution to my dilemma and my folks were for me in it. I could even think about the bike I was riding and the special meaning it held for me. There hadn't been much opportunity for those memories to surface lately. How I got that bike may just show something about what could happen—even at age ten—when Brooks Robinson made his mind up about something.

There was a bubble-gum-blowing contest on a Saturday at Lamar Porter Field, and it seemed like every kid at Woodruff Grammar School had entered. As I left I announced, "I'm going to walk, Mom. I can't ride two bikes home, and I'm going to win a new one in the bubble-gum-blowing contest."

But when I got there, I was almost overwhelmed to see all those contestants. Seeing the size of the bubbles being blown up by some of my friends and hearing the announcer report how big those bubbles were made me begin to wonder. I hadn't ever faced a really competitive challenge like this before.

The bikes were up on stage. They were bright red. One for a boy, one for a girl. They had those big black balloon tires—not the thin kind you see for the ten-speeds that are so popular now. Every kid in the contest wanted to win one, but I just knew I was going to. I'd walked.

Finally it was my turn. I was down near the end of the list of contestants. I'd chewed a lot of gum, just because I liked it, not to practice. (Mom always claims that the reason I had to have braces on my teeth about this time was because I'd pushed them out blowing so many bubbles.) I was given the one stick of Bub gum allotted to every contestant, instructed to chew it to the consistency I wanted, and then allowed to do my thing.

I took a couple of deep breaths, got just as much air into my lungs as I could, and started blowing.

You had to hold the bubble long enough for the judges to measure it. I remember exactly what they said when they announced the size of mine: "Brooks Robinson, ten and three-eighths inches, to take the lead."

A few minutes later it was all over. Mayor Sam Wassell crowned me and Arlene Turner as King and Queen Bub. I didn't even mind that Arlene was the best because her bubble measured twelve and a sixteenth inches. When I rode home the mile or so from Porter Field on that shiny new red bike, I was the happiest ten-year-old in all of Arkansas. But I guess the happiest person of all was Mom when she saw me riding up the hill to the house.

The next day as I was flopping the papers I happened to catch a headline: "374 Enter Bubblegum Contest." The article went on: "Brooks Robinson and Arlene Turner were crowned King and Queen Bub by Mayor Sam Wassell yesterday afternoon after winning the titles over 372 other contestants at Lamar Porter Field.

"Robinson, 10, of 2012 Lloyd Court won by blowing a bubble $10\frac{3}{8}$ inches around for which he received a Monarch bicycle presented by the Bowman Gum Corporation. Arlene Turner surpassed Brooks with a bubble $12\frac{1}{16}$ inches big and also won a bicycle."

Now whether or not that was my first press clipping I

can't remember, but it was the biggest thing that had happened to me until then. And it sticks in my memory that you've got to have a certain confidence about you whenever you're challenged in a contest, whether it's blowing bubbles or hitting baseballs.

5

When I entered Little Rock Senior as a tenth grader, it was the main high school in town—with probably three thousand students—and those of us in sports seemed to know everyone on campus. We played in a tough conference—the Big Seven. The name meant just that. Included were the seven largest schools in Arkansas at the time: Fort Smith, Pine Bluff, Hot Springs, El Dorado, North Little Rock, Texarkana, and Little Rock Senior. Our conference competition was limited to football, basketball, and track. Standard policy then—and still today—was for major schools in the state with football programs not to have baseball teams. Consequently, in Little Rock, Legion ball was the only organized baseball program for teenage players.

Since I was sticking with the decision I'd already made

not to play football, I turned to basketball my first year as a way of keeping in shape until time for the Legion baseball season. Practice at Little Rock Senior didn't start when school opened in September, but I started working out anyway. Here again Dad was always ready to help me out. He'd built a goal in the back yard for me when I first showed an interest in basketball, and we made good use of it for one-on-one and free-throw-shooting contests. I learned a lot too, because Dad had lettered for Little Rock Senior as a guard, the same position I played.

It was tough trying to make the team as a tenth grader, even though Winston Faulkner, my junior high coach, who was now assistant to George Haynie, knew what I could do. Most of my playing was on the junior varsity, but as about the eleventh or twelfth man I still got to travel with the varsity except when tournament time came. Then we were restricted to ten men, and I couldn't go.

I'll never forget our first game that year. Well into the second half, a lot of my sophomore classmates began to chant, "We want Brooks, we want Brooks." When I realized what they were doing all I wanted to do was find a hole in that hardwood.

Coach Haynie was sitting beside me. "Sounds like you've got a fan club, Brooks," he commented.

"Guess they're trying to tell you something, Coach," I recall replying.

A minute or two after that he put me in. That might not have happened if we'd been playing fast break all the time. Coach was always giving me a bad time about my speed. Fortunately for me, our game was more pattern basketball.

The first time we came down the floor the play call gave me the option of cutting off the center. I made an unreal shot. The ball came off the backboard to the floor; I hit it

[34]

almost like a dribble; the ball bounced up, hit the board, and spun in. My friends in the stands nearly brought the place down. It was a great basket.

"Put the Round Man in!" became a pretty common call at the games after that. Because I was a bit pudgy then I had gotten tagged with that name when I first got to high school and on the basketball team. But though that yell always brought a smile to Haynie, it didn't get me in the game very often that first year.

During my next two years, however, I was a regular starter. Our team did well when I was a junior although we weren't big. The tallest man we had was Harry Vines, who must have been about six four or five. But, solid as we were, Jonesboro was probably the greatest team ever to come out of Arkansas in those years, and they beat us twice during the season—once by a point at Little Rock and once by a large margin at Jonesboro. Then we got them in the state tournament. Down by ten points or so, we put on a rally, caught them, and went ahead with a two-point lead.

Before we knew it, we had lost the chance to put the game out of sight. Two missed layups, one of them mine, blotted us out of the picture. So close and yet so far! Having the opportunity to do the job and blowing it remains one of the bleakest moments of my life.

One of the biggest messes I ever got into was with some of my basketball teammates. One night we'd been to the Minuteman, a hamburger place on Broadway near the Roxie and Rex theaters, when someone suggested we have a little fun up on "Lovers Lane." That was on Palisades Drive, a cul de sac where they were building some new houses—a favorite place for teenagers to go and park. We rolled some big boulders out across the road to block the cars in. Just as we finished a police car rolled up.

Lining us up against the car, one of them began questioning us. "What's your name?" he started with me.

"Brooks Robinson, sir," I choked out.

"Oh, your dad's a fireman, isn't he?"

"Yes, sir."

"What's your name?" he turned to Rotenberry.

"Buddy Rotenberry," he replied.

"Wasn't your grandfather the police chief a few years back?"

"Yes, sir."

We all thought we were going to jail, but after we'd rolled the boulders off the road they sent us home fearing the worst if our parents found out. They never did, but I was really worried for a long time that we might be kicked off the basketball team or, worse yet, Dad would really crack down on me.

As it turned out, though, over those last two years I averaged sixteen or seventeen points a game and had been named twice to All-Big-Seven and to one All-State first team. An old scrapbook of Dad's from the '30s which I'd discovered when I was very small may have had something to do with that. I was constantly comparing clippings about Dad's basketball career with what I had done, and his excellent record must have spurred me on considerably, I realize now.

That scrapbook also made clear to me what it must have cost Dad to hide his disappointment at my not going out for high school football. He was a letterman in that sport too—a quarterback—and several of his old clippings indicate he must have been a pretty good passer. I'm glad my brother, Gary, made such a name for himself in Little Rock football. He was an outstanding back for Little Rock Central, and he gave us all a thrill returning the opening kickoff for a touchdown in the Thanksgiving Day game his senior year.

Gary, who is five years younger than I, went on to play wingback and defensive back on a football scholarship for the University of Arkansas, where my old high school coach, Wilson Matthews, was an assistant to Coach Frank Broyles. I had had the opportunity to go to Arkansas too, on a four-year basketball scholarship, but rejected it in spite of head basketball coach Glen Rose's strong arguments. He had talked to a scout who'd predicted I'd never make it to the major leagues, and he tried to convince me that my basketball skills would enable me to get an education at Arkansas while at the same time I might improve my baseball skills even more in college ball than in the minor leagues.

But, much as I enjoyed basketball, it was never higher than second place with me. Springtime and Legion ball were what I really lived for. Anything else I did in between seasons was for one purpose—to stay in shape. In my senior year that obsession pushed me to new lengths. We had just played our last basketball game when George Haynie asked me what I was going to do in the weeks remaining before Legion ball. When I replied that I hadn't given it much thought, he came back at me with a real shocker. "What you ought to do," he told me, "is go run track."

I looked at him kind of funny because the last guy in the world to be on a track team was Brooks Robinson. Fast I wasn't. Quick, yes—but I didn't think there was much of a place on that cinder oval for a guy who wasn't fast.

Wanting to improve my speed as much as possible, however, I followed Haynie's advice. And after watching me work out a day or two, Don Sparks, the track coach, called

[37]

me over. "You're no sprinter, Brooks," he pronounced, "but you've got a nice long stride and you run hard. Doing a lot of long sprint work will get you in top shape for baseball and you can probably score some points for us in the eight-eighty."

"Coach," I said, stunned, "you just told me I'm not a sprinter and that I know. Then you tell me you want me to run the eight-eighty. That's almost a sprint for anyone but me. For me it might as well be a mile."

Coach Sparks finally convinced me to give it a try. And much to my amazement, when running the third leg on a relay against Fort Smith, I beat my opponent by a considerable distance. My teammates told me I won the relay for them, but I still feel my competition must have been mighty slow.

My best time in the eight-eighty—2:05—wouldn't even get you a suit now, but in those days the state record was two flat, held by Wayne Young, a fellow who was a year behind me at Little Rock Senior. And it doesn't matter that school history doesn't show me as much of a track man. When it was time to play baseball again, I was in the greatest shape of my life.

Chapter 6

I got my start in Legion ball when I wasn't quite fifteen, playing for the M. M. Eberts Post No. 1 Doughboys, the same team my dad had played for years before. George Haynie was the coach, and it must have been out of friendship for my dad that he kept me on the squad that first year, even though I was pretty good with the glove. I was younger and smaller than any other kid going out for the team, and I had to really get into a ball with my bat before my hitting had any drive to it.

It was midsummer before I got into a game. We were over at Altus, Oklahoma, and we were getting clobbered by the local team in the first round of the annual Tri-State Fourth of July Legion tournament. Altus was loaded with talent. Lindy McDaniel, later a relief pitcher for the New York Yankees and now with the Kansas City Royals, and

Eddie Fisher, who has been pitching for thirteen or four-teen years in the big leagues, were both regular pitchers for them.

McDaniel was on the mound that day, and he wasn't giving us anything. Late in the game, Haynie turned toward me. "Brooksie," he said, "go up there and get me a hit."

He must have stunned me. I didn't make a move until one of the guys beside me on the bench nudged me that George wanted me to bat. When I got a double almost down the line into left field, I was the most excited kid in Okla-homa and Arkansas and Texas, all three.

Otherwise, that first year with the Eberts Post wasn't very happy for me. Our record wasn't good enough for us to make the playoffs and I found it pretty tough sitting on the bench most of the time. During the winter, however, I grew a bit, and by the time for spring practice I was about five six or so and maybe a hundred and forty-five pounds. That added size seemed to give more power to my hitting—at least that's what I'd tell Dad when he had time to pitch extra batting practice to me.

We were a much better club in 1952. And it was better for me because I was playing regularly. Haynie had me at third, where I felt most comfortable. I lacked the range to be a good shortstop, and at second base there was the problem of having to be quick on the pivot or getting wiped out.

We seemed to have all the marks of a good team. Our infield was tight; we had good pitching; another year of growing had helped a lot of the younger players; and we'd all gained a lot of experience the year before, even though it was the first time in ten years that we hadn't made the state Legion tournament.

Nevertheless, we suffered some bitter disappointments.

The first came in July in the deciding game of a double elimination affair, the annual Tri-State Tournament at Altus. Amazingly, we had defeated the host Altus Harvesters in the first round to break a 31-game winning streak for them. But after losing in our second game, we had to defeat Altus again in a crucial third contest, and we fell short. It was a long ride home—a lot longer than those five hundred miles had seemed when we were covering them in the other direction, dreaming of a championship—and conversation was at a minimum. As we approached Little Rock's suburbs on what was then U.S. 64, George Haynie stood up. "Practice tomorrow, twelve-thirty," he announced, and he didn't have to waste any words. "Everyone be on time."

When the bus dropped us off at Lamar Porter Field, we all quietly began to find our ways home. After being consoled by both my parents, I headed back to Lamar Porter Field with Dad. By the time we reached the field, several of the other guys were there too. With Dad hitting infield to us we went through a workout on our own. More than anything else, it seemed to relieve the tension of that long ride back in the bus.

We'd been working about half an hour or so when George Haynie drove up. He always seemed to appear after we'd had a big letdown like this one. As darkness closed in and the impromptu practice began to break up, I walked over to where Haynie and Dad were standing.

"We'll make the playoffs," I said, as much to reassure myself as to make a promise to Coach Haynie.

Sure enough, as the season wore on, we began to gather momentum, putting together two or three good win streaks. Going into the regionals we had a 24–8 mark, and my batting average was up over .300.

We opened with Lonoke, a town the first stop east of

Little Rock, and beat them, 19–1. Then we continued a hot hitting streak by clobbering Pine Bluff, 13–5. In a later round of play, however, Pine Bluff beat us in fourteen innings, and that called for a sudden-death go with Pine Bluff. Win, we'd move up; lose and it would be another of those bus rides, only this time from Pine Bluff rather than Altus.

Pine Bluff took a lead into the eighth inning. They were up, 5–3, a pitcher named Joe Marks having blanked us from about the second inning on. Finally in the eighth we got the bases loaded, partly on a single by me. Then Marks hit Tommy Lauderdale, and it was 5–4.

That brought Ashley up. As he singled into right to score two runs, the throw from the outfield went wild, allowing Lauderdale to score and Ashley to reach third. Before the inning was over, we'd scored six runs and won the district title, 9–5. That put us into the state finals.

The next week, we bused to Newport, Arkansas—a town about a hundred miles or so northeast of Little Rock— where we took two games in a row and the state title. John Venable, a big righthander with a fine fast ball, threw a no-hitter in the first game, winning 6–0. He came back two days later to win again, 4–1.

Our next stop was the regional championship. Billed for Ponchatoula, Louisiana, it matched teams from Texas, Louisiana, Mississippi, and Arkansas. We made it all the way to the finals before losing to Austin, Texas, 3–2.

It was another long, long bus ride back to Little Rock. But as we covered the miles with George Haynie doing a lot of the driving and talking to each of us when he wasn't at the wheel, we began to remember how far we'd come since our first game in June.

I remember remarking to one of my teammates, "Nobody figured we'd do this well."

When I came in the door at home, Dad was there to meet me. More than anything else, I guess, he was there to console me because he knew how hard I took defeat.

"It was a pretty good year. We all learned a lot, and I learned a lot about hitting—how to spray the ball around and how to wait for my pitch. But the most important thing I learned," I admitted to Dad, "it's a lot more fun to win than to lose."

Chapter 7

Pro baseball scouts were always around Legion ball. But in 1953, after the outstanding showing we made in the annual 4th of July tournament at Altus, there seemed to be more of them than usual. Perhaps it was all in my imagination, or perhaps a letter one of Dad's friends wrote in my behalf may have had something to do with it.

Before the season began I'd been worried about what kind of showing I'd make, because I'd known for some time that Coach Haynie had plans for me to be his first second baseman. Although I didn't like the idea, I realized his problem and was resigned to having to handle that spot. But when Harold Ellingson, who had been tabbed for third —his best position—broke his collarbone just before we really got going, I was sure I'd be going back there after all.

My hopes were soon dashed. During a workout one afternoon when we were taking infield and I was on third, Coach Haynie called me over. Never one to beat around the bush, he came right to the point. "I know your heart is set on playing third, Brooks, and you're our best third baseman, but you're also the only one we've got who can make the double-play pivot at second. If you play second, we've got a big problem solved. Then I can play C. B. Newton over on third and we'd have a pretty solid infield."

My disappointment must have been obvious even while I was assuring the coach it didn't matter where I played just so long as we had the best team possible.

"Third is your position," he acknowledged. "We both know that. We also know that the scouts are coming around looking at you and we want you to look your best. But we've got to be solid down the middle or none of us will look good to anyone."

As usual, the best forecast of our season would be our play in the Tri-State tournament at Altus. We were all optimistic, but things looked pretty black when we lost to the host team in the first round. But then we took Memphis, 15–4, and held on in a return game with Altus to edge them out, 7–6.

Topeka, the lone unbeaten team in the tournament, was our next hurdle. Coming up in the losers' bracket, we'd have to take Topeka in a doubleheader if we were going to win the title. We bombed them out in the opener, 12–9, but taking the title was a tight affair with a 3–2 score. All in all, it was one of my better tournaments, especially the final doubleheader. I had two doubles and a single in the first game and a double and a single in the finals.

The next Sunday as my parents and Gary and I were leaving Capitol View Methodist Church after the service, Lindsay Deal, a longtime friend of Dad's, came up to talk.

Mr. Deal, who had played either with or for Paul Richards in Atlanta in the old Southern Association, was at all our games. He told my dad that he had written a letter to Richards, then the field manager and general manager of the Baltimore Orioles, suggesting that perhaps their organization might like to take a look at me.

That really impressed me. I knew no one could sign me until after I graduated from high school, but for Mr. Deal to feel that I was already good enough to have someone from the Orioles take a look at me gave me hope that maybe my dreams could be realized.

"Dear Paul," wrote Mr. Deal to Richards.

"I am writing to you in regard to a youngster named Brooks Robinson. I think he measures up to having a chance in major league baseball. I think he is a natural third baseman although he has been playing both second and third. . . .

"He is no speed demon but neither is he a truck horse. I believe in a year or two he will be above average in speed. He hit well over .400 in American Legion baseball, including all tournament games. At the tournament in Altus, Oklahoma, he was awarded the trophy for being the outstanding player.

"Brooks has a lot of power, baseball savvy, and is always cool when the chips are down. This boy is the best prospect I've seen since Billy Goodman came to Atlanta to play when I was playing there. . . ."

Lindsay was genuinely interested in seeing that I got the best deal possible in baseball. And by writing directly to Paul Richards as a personal friend, he felt he would at least get my name up to the top where it wouldn't get lost in the organization.

I remember Dad telling me on the way home from

church, "Buddy, there will be scouts around every time you play. Just remember, play each game as it comes. Don't worry about scouts being in the stands. Just do your best every time."

"It won't bother me," I responded. "I'm too busy during a game. All I can think about is making the plays as they come to me."

We were a good team. We went through the regular season that year losing only three games out of nineteen, and we took the Arkansas state Legion title by beating El Dorado on their field, 2–0. Robert Nosari, our pitcher, and a little guy for the job, nearly had a no-hitter until the ninth when he allowed two men to get on with two men out.

We got as far as the finals of the regional series in Ponchatoula, Louisiana, but lost to Monroe. Ending the season with a long bus ride back after a defeat wasn't exactly what we'd hoped for, but there were still plenty of good memories to carry us through the winter.

When school began in September, I turned my thinking to basketball. A great year for our team, including getting to the state finals, made the time pass quickly. But when we'd finished that season and the weather began to turn a little warm, I couldn't wait to get out on Lamar Porter Field or the Deaf School practice lot and play some baseball.

Things were different this year. For the first time since I was a kid, George Haynie wasn't going to be around. He'd taken a job with Johnson & Johnson, the firm that makes bandages and adhesive tape, and was traveling throughout the Southwest as representative to various high schools and colleges.

A lot of the older kids were gone too. Ernie Tabor had signed with the Phillies. Lawrence Stolzer had gone to the University of Arkansas on a baseball scholarship and the

[47]

Dodgers had signed Charlie Callaway. It was going to be a rebuilding year. From the coach on down, there were a lot of new faces, and Woody Johnson, who had taken over for Haynie, had a tough job ahead.

That we had problems was obvious in our opening game. But although we lost to North Little Rock, 4–2, my home run over the left field fence, one of the longest shots in my Legion baseball career, provided a bright spot for me.

When it came time for our long trip to Altus and the annual 4th of July tournament, we seemed to be pretty well together. Our infield had meshed into a unit, and I was even called on to pitch from time to time. In the semifinals of the tournament I went the distance with Altus, and my five-hitter—a game in which I also got three hits, one of them a long home run—eliminated them, 18–6.

We won our second consecutive championship the next day by defeating Topeka, 8–7. It gave me great satisfaction to win the game with a triple that cleaned the bases for our one-run margin.

That was probably as good a series as I had in all my American Legion baseball career. Named the most valuable player in the tournament, I had a .647 batting average and twelve runs batted in. That bus ride back home seemed one of the shortest ever, especially when I kept looking at the trophy I had received.

Our trip to the finals of the Arkansas American Legion tournament was another story. We all wanted to win so we'd get another shot at the regionals, and, we hoped, a chance to play for the national championship—the World Series of Legion baseball. But our dreams went up in smoke when we lost to El Dorado. Even though I went three for four that day, I was thoroughly dejected as I walked off the field to the clubhouse.

Efforts to comfort me by one of the scouts at the game were to no avail. "Don't feel too bad," he said. "You played well and you gave it all you had."

All I could think of was that we lost, the first time that had happened to Little Rock in the state championship in years. How many, I don't remember, but quite some number, and to make it worse, this was my last game for the American Legion, even though I still had my senior year of high school ahead of me. I'd be graduating next May, and either I'd have it made with a baseball contract or I'd be going on to take that baseball and basketball scholarship to the University of Arkansas.

As the school year moved along and Little Rock Senior became Central High, more and more time was spent trying to evaluate my plans for the future. Sometimes I seemed to be living in a dream world. We had endless family conferences at the dinner table or after some scout had come by to talk with us. There was never any real change in my thinking—only a few misgivings. But when you're seventeen and torn between a pro career and college, that's to be expected.

"You have to do what you want to do, Brooks," Mom reluctantly told me again one night during a prolonged after-dinner discussion.

"I want to play baseball," I responded firmly, "more than anything else."

"That's what it should be then," Dad supported me, knowing full well that Mom still wanted me to go to Arkansas. "But not many boys get a chance at a four-year scholarship." Dad went on doing his best to pacify both of us. "You could wait until after college to try pro ball."

Deep down, though, I was afraid that I might get hurt playing basketball or baseball at Arkansas and that might end my hopes to play in the majors. "I can go to school during the off-season," I argued.

So it was decided for about the fiftieth time that if everything fell into place, I would sign a professional contract. I was confident I was ready if one of the many clubs that had talked to me during the winter made the right offer. Then it would be pro baseball for sure.

Chapter 8

Graduation ceremonies for my senior class were held on the night of May 28, 1955. The president of the senior class, Richard Bell, to whom I'd lost in the election for that office and who is now a football coach at Texas Tech, was going to make the class address. We'd rehearsed everything for an outdoor ceremony at the football stadium, so, of course, it rained—so hard that even when we moved inside, the stage was almost like a lake from water coming through the roof in the old gym. It was a nice affair, I suppose. But to tell the truth, I was so nervous about the next day I can't recall much else of what went on.

For most teenagers high school graduation was the biggest thing in life to that point. It never really was for me. Unlike most of the gang, who went off on a big all-night celebration at country clubs and private homes, I spent a quiet evening with my parents and Gary. With Dad's help, a number of appointments to talk with baseball scouts had been set up beginning early the next morning.

During the months after my last Legion season we'd listened to offers from seven or eight clubs. The possibilities had narrowed down to probably three of them; the Cincinnati Reds, the New York Giants, and Baltimore. We'd figured things every way possible and decided that I wanted to sign a major league contract, but not a bonus contract unless they offered me over $30,000.

Actually, if they had offered $30,000, I would have taken it. It was pretty well known that I wasn't going to get a large offer. I didn't have those super qualities they were looking for—speed, size, strength and the other pluses they want in a bonus ball player. We had decided we'd pass any lower offers because it wouldn't be worth it to lose the experience. What I really wanted was that major league contract instead of a minor league.

Back in 1955 if a player signed a bonus contract, anything over $4,000, he had to go directly to the major leagues. That I didn't want; I knew I wasn't ready for the majors. But, on the other hand, I didn't want to sign a minor league agreement because that meant the club had control of me for six years. A minor league contract allowed three options in the minors; after that, once the player made the majors the parent club had three more options. If you signed a major league contract to begin with, all the club had was three options on you and then someone else had a chance to pick you up.

Detroit talked to us a lot but insisted on a minor league contract. They told me they'd send me to a Class B club— probably Panama City—but there was no way they'd sign me to a major league agreement. So, we eliminated them from our thinking.

We didn't really know how to handle the whole thing since it was all new to us. The best solution Dad could reach was to give each representative forty-five minutes to make his final offer the next day, May 29. We met them all in the living room in the big white two-story house on Denison Street. Mom had made coffee, and a fair amount of it must have been consumed as we heard each man out.

As I recall, Hugh Poland, the scout assigned by the New York Giants to try and sign me, was the first to appear. Poland, who had seen me work out several times with the Travelers, said his club was willing to give me a $4,000 salary, but not a major league contract.

Next came Paul Florence, representing the Cincinnati Reds. Florence offered a major league contract and a $4,000 salary, which was just about what Dad and I had expected. After he had outlined the Reds' offer and explained in some detail what they planned for me in their development program, Baltimore's turn came.

Art Ehlers had been sent from Baltimore by Paul Richards to sign me. The Orioles had shown more interest, so far as I could determine, than anyone else. Several times Richards had sent Claude Dietrich, one of his scouts, out to watch me play. Then Fred Hoffman, another scout for Baltimore, swung by and watched me in my final Legion season. If I remember correctly, out of the sixteen major league clubs that were in existence then, ten or eleven talked to me, some a lot more than others, and Baltimore more than anyone else.

Now it was down to Cincinnati and Baltimore, and Ehlers arrived at the house at the precise hour. That impressed me. I like people to be prompt.

We talked a great deal and Ehlers outlined again the Baltimore proposal.

"We'd like very much to sign you," I remember him telling us. "Us" included Mom, Dad, Gary, and me. We were all gathered around the coffee table in the living room listening to each man and, most intently, to Ehlers.

"But we have to be honest with you, Brooks. We can't give you a bonus. We'll give you a major league contract and $4,000 salary. To be frank with you," Ehlers continued, "we are more interested in giving a large bonus to a youngster named Wayne Causey from Monroe, Louisiana."

I knew Wayne Causey. The Legion team had played against Monroe in the regionals at Ponchatoula twice.

"He's a good player," I remember telling Ehlers.

"We think so, too," Ehlers asserted. "We have a scout down at his home right now signing him." That information must have caused me to show a little outward concern because Ehlers added: "I hope that doesn't upset you. I just wanted you to know all the details before we went on."

It didn't really bother me. I knew Causey was considered a top prospect in Legion ball and was going to go for a big bonus—maybe $35,000 or so. Causey's credentials were superior to mine in just about every department. It's no wonder he was offered a lot more money. Judging a young ball player is difficult—risky, to say the least. Some fellows mature quicker than others and I just didn't have the maturity a Wayne Causey did at that stage in our careers. He was stronger physically and did everything just a little better than I did.

The way it turned out, the agreement we reached was the best thing that could have happened to me. Going down and playing with guys my own speed, I really got my feet on the ground, whereas Causey just had to be thrown directly into big league action. While there was no great pressure at the time in Baltimore, still, Wayne was in over his head. I might have been in the same situation, or worse.

Ehlers revealed Baltimore's combined scouting report on me. "They've given you a better than average overall rating," said Ehlers. "Your low mark is a C in running. You're a fine fielder and you've got a good arm. In general we feel you have both the physical tools we seek and the right attitude."

Once more Ehlers confirmed that the most they could offer me was $4,000 and a major league contract. "If you show what we think you will in the minors," he pointed out, "we'll move you up fast. With us, you have the chance to move up faster than with probably any other club."

My mind was already made up, but Mr. Ehlers excused himself, saying he'd be waiting at the hotel for our decision. We told him we wanted to think about it overnight and promised that by midmorning of Memorial Day we'd give him our answer.

When Ehlers had gone, we sat around and talked things over for a couple of hours. Baltimore was it, and probably the clinching argument was Paul Richards. He'd shown an interest ever since Lindsay Deal had written the letter about me. We had talked on the phone once or twice, and I still remember his words.

"Look, son," Richards declared, "if you've got anything on the ball, you're going to be able to play here quicker because we've got no young ball players at all. We're just starting out in Baltimore, and this is your best opportunity in baseball to play in the major leagues."

Everything about the Baltimore offer appealed to me. It fit the things Dad and I wanted. They were in need of young players. They had no solid third baseman and even though most of my Legion career had been at second base and that's where Baltimore was going to start me, deep down I believed that my future rested at third.

And with all those words, all that talk, and all that con-
fusion of listening to men offer contracts to a young teenage prospect, all I wanted to do was get to bed and to sleep
so I could wake up on Memorial Day morning and get to
that telephone.

Memorial Day was bright and clear and really quiet when I woke up. This was the day I'd waited for and dreamed about ever since I could remember.

After breakfast, around nine o'clock, I began my telephone calls. The first was to Hugh Poland, who had known all along that the Giants didn't have much of a chance because of their low offer.

Then I called Paul Florence, whom I'd grown to like quite well, at his hotel. When he answered, I informed him that although my decision was to sign with Baltimore, I wanted to tell him of it personally and express my gratitude for all his consideration and attention.

He thanked me for calling. "Not many boys let us know," he said. "I appreciate the call and wish you the best of luck."

Then I dialed Mr. Ehlers's hotel. When he came on the line, I fairly blurted out, "I'm going to sign with Baltimore." He said that was fine and that he would come over to our house in a little while with a contract. And to my surprise, he suggested that I begin to pack because he wanted to leave on the afternoon plane.

Suddenly everything began to seem unreal, now that I was about to sign and head for Baltimore. Ehlers had outlined what was in store for me in the way of competition for infield positions in the years ahead. Causey had been signed in the hope that he could handle the third-base job. Baltimore had also signed Jim Pyburn, an All-American football player from Auburn University. Chuck Diering, who was really an outfielder, had even played some third for them.

While I was laying out my one suit, shirts, sweaters, and shoes to be packed into a single suitcase, along with my spikes and glove, Mom kept coming into the room. I knew she was upset, not about my signing, but about my leaving home.

"Brooks, you'll be going away for a long time," she said, "so you'd better use the big suitcase."

We'd packed many times before for road trips with the Legion team and I'd always used the small one. When Mom said that, it dawned on me for the first time that I wouldn't be coming home in a few days, but, if all went well, something more like six months.

The thought shook me. I'd been away to Altus and Ponchatoula and places like that for tournaments and play-offs. But six months—that was kind of scary. Gary was helping me pack, and as things went into the bag I became more and more emotional. I realized then just how important your mom and dad and brother are to you. They are always there when you need them, and right now I needed all the consolation and affection they could give me.

Just about then the doorbell rang. It was somewhere between ten and ten-thirty. Art Ehlers, a smile on his face, had arrived, ready to sign me. We all went into the living room and cleared off the coffee table. With my parents beside me and Gary looking over our shoulders, I signed my first baseball contract. I was eighteen years and twelve days old. After Dad countersigned for me, Ehlers picked up his copies of the contract, carefully tucked them into his briefcase, and then shook hands all around. "We're on the afternoon plane to Baltimore," Ehlers confirmed.

As we all drove to Little Rock airport in the blue Nash, the car I learned to drive in, every bump seemed to jar me back to reality. I noticed that Mom's eyes were moist and that Gary was swallowing all the time. All I could do was look out the window. I wasn't as grown up as I thought.

After Mr. Ehlers had checked us in and our luggage had been taken away, we did our best to make small talk until the call to board the plane boomed out over the speaker system. Then all the family sentiment came spilling forth.

Gary gave me a hug and a good luck wish.

Dad shook hands with me, man to man, then impulsively gave me a bear hug that nearly popped my back. "Good luck, Brooks," he said to me, his voice a little unsteady. I think that's the first time Dad ever called me Brooks. It was always Buddy before.

Mom was all tears when I kissed her good-by. "Remember," she warned me, "you write. Write often."

As we walked out to the plane, I turned around a time or two to wave to the folks. Then all at once the awareness

[59]

that I was on my own hit me with full force. There was no one to talk to when a problem arose. I'd have to buy my own food and clothes and pay all my own bills.

I'd calculated that my $4,000 contract, based on a six months season, would come out to $666 per month. That seemed like a fortune to me. But I soon found out that when you're paying your board and room and all the incidental things you'd never noticed before, it doesn't go very far.

Before that first season was over, I found out all about the problems of taxes and investigations too. Cincinnati protested my signing with Baltimore to Commissioner Ford Frick. Gabe Paul, then the Reds' general manager, felt there had been some under-the-table dealings.

In Lynchburg, Virginia, one day, when I was playing with York, a fellow from Frick's office came to see me and asked about the details of my signing. Then shortly after that, word came from Baltimore that Paul Richards, Claude Dietrich, and I had to go to Frick's office for a hearing on my signing.

You can imagine what went through my mind as I was ushered into Frick's office alone, asked to sit down and then to swear on a Bible "to tell the truth, the whole truth, and nothing but the truth."

Frick went over every detail of my signing from the first time I talked with Lindsay Deal until I signed the contract on that Memorial Day morning with Art Ehlers. Richards and Dietrich went in separately, too, but nothing ever came of the hearing, as far as the Commissioner of Baseball was concerned.

It was another story, however, with the commissioner of the Internal Revenue Service. One day an IRS agent came around to see me. An investigation of my taxes had just been initiated, he informed me.

Can you imagine that! Here I was, an eighteen-year-old who'd probably received a total of a thousand dollars by then, and already the IRS was looking into my taxes! It seems that they had a report that I had signed for a $4,000 bonus and $4,000 annual salary. Finally, after talking to me and the Orioles' management, they decided their report was wrong. I never heard any more about it.

If I'd had any idea I'd be facing such things in my first two months in baseball, I'd have been terrified that May afternoon when I climbed onto the plane with Ehlers. But even though this was the first commercial flight I'd ever been on, I wasn't at all perturbed. At eighteen you take things in stride.

We hadn't been airborne ten minutes before I fell asleep. I must have been exhausted from all the excitement of graduation and the signing, because I didn't realize until later that it was quite a bumpy trip. Ehlers knew it; he didn't sleep at all.

"Are you always this relaxed?" he wanted to know after we had landed. It was night in Baltimore and the lights of the city seemed to make a gigantic glittering carpet over the area as we came into the airport.

"I didn't know whether I was going to be afraid or not," I explained, "so I decided to go to sleep. I had a good rest," I added. Ehlers acknowledged, almost resentfully, that it had seemed that way to him, too.

Ehlers took me in a cab to the Southern Hotel, not far from Baltimore Memorial Stadium. After getting me registered and asking the clerk to bill the club, he said he would see me tomorrow.

"Be at the park about 5:00 P.M. We'll give you a uniform then. Be sure and get a good night's sleep."

I did. The following morning I got up early, dressed, and

took a walk around town. I don't even remember where I had breakfast, but it wasn't in the hotel. I recall going to a movie at a theater up on Howard Street and having lunch about midafternoon at the Oriole Cafeteria. The name didn't make an impact on me. But, when I hailed a cab and asked the driver to take me to the Orioles' ball park, I discovered it was just around the corner. I could have walked.

After wandering around the outside of the stadium for a while I saw the sign: "Players' Entrance."

That simply painted sign had all the glamor of a brilliantly lighted theater marquee for me. Here I was, Brooks Robinson, Jr., walking into a major league clubhouse as a player. It didn't matter that in a few days I'd be going down to the minors; part of my enduring childhood dream had been realized.

When I walked in and asked for Mr. Ehlers, one of the clubhouse boys directed me over to an office where he was sitting with John Lancaster, the Orioles' traveling secretary. The two of them took me into Paul Richards's office.

Richards—a tall, thin man with square jaw, tan complexion, and wavy grey hair—matched the many pictures I had seen of him over the years. What the pictures hadn't shown was his hard, clear eyes.

Richards had taken over at Baltimore in 1954 as field manager and general manager. Many still regard Paul as one of the most astute men in baseball when it comes to building a franchise and developing young players. He was as trim in manner as in physical appearance—all business and right to the point.

"We'll keep you with us for a few days," he told me, "and take you along on our next trip so you can see what life is like in baseball. Then we'll send you down to our

[62]

Class B club at York in the Piedmont League." His words reinforced what Ehlers had told me on our way to Baltimore and what had been stated in various conversations before my signing.

"All right?" Richards put the rhetorical question. Without waiting for my reply, he instructed me to get a uniform, take some grounders, and, before all the regulars had batting practice, to hit a little.

Putting on the Baltimore uniform for the first time sent chills tingling up and down my spine. Even when I put on that cap with the Oriole on it and checked in the mirror, I couldn't quite believe that the reflection staring back at me was Brooks Robinson. But as I went out to the field, it was no trouble at all to convince myself that everything surely was right with the world on this nice Tuesday afternoon in Maryland.

When I came down the final steps of the tunnel to the dugout and then out into the light of day, I stopped for just a second. There they were, the Baltimore Orioles, and here I was, one of them. If it hadn't been for the uniforms, I'd have had to pinch myself. In my childhood dreams there was a different color bird on my cap—a redbird—and I was making like Stan Musial of the St. Louis Cardinals.

Baltimore didn't have any Stan Musial then but there were a lot of names that brought instant recognition—Gene Woodling, Billy Cox, Joe Coleman, Sr., Bob Nieman, Hoot Evers, and Gus Triandos, a giant of a catcher who'd also come from the Yanks. There was Chuck Diering, also, a legitimate outfielder who had been playing a little third.

They were all names I used to follow every day in the *Gazette* back home to see how they'd done the day before. I used to devour the major league box scores in Little Rock. I knew almost to the man what everyone had done, espe-

[63]

cially the Orioles, since I'd pretty well made up my mind to sign with them long before that became an actuality.

Maybe some of these fellows were going down, but to me they were among the giants of baseball. Nothing in the world would ever be quite like this particular hour in my life.

Finally breaking loose from the enchantment, I jumped up the steps of the dugout and trotted out onto the field of Memorial Stadium. Probably it was no better grass than hundreds of other diamonds in the country but on this day it felt like green velvet to me. I ran a little in the outfield just to get loosened up and then gradually worked my way in toward the infield to field some grounders while the non-starters were hitting.

As I moved onto the field, one of the coaches, Al Vincent, began to hit grounders to me. At first they were easy hoppers almost in my glove. Always they came right after the batter in the cage had hit so that the infielders could be alert for their hits and not get hurt. Almost imperceptibly the tempo of the ground balls from Vincent picked up. They were sharper, harder to handle, first on one side and then on the other. Each time they stretched me out a little more, but I handled them and fired them all over to first base.

If I never got any farther in baseball than just this drill, I thought, a lot of my dreams and ambitions had already been realized. I wasn't willing to settle for that, really, but it sure was something being out there with the Orioles, fielding grounders as the spectators slowly began to file into the stadium.

"Robinson," someone called out. I looked around to see if there was another. "You'd better get in the cage and hit some."

One of the coaches, Harry Brecheen, was throwing batting practice, and I lined his first pitch into left. The next one I slashed to the right of second into center field and I could tell it had been hit well by the sound from the bat. I probably hit three or four more balls before they yelled me out of the cage.

Baltimore's road trip began the next day, with the first stop in Cleveland. Being excess baggage didn't keep me from enjoying the experience. I took a lot of infield, got to hit some and even threw a little batting practice. Richards had roomed me with Hoot Evers, a tall blond of about six-two who was in his first season with Baltimore after having been a regular for Detroit. Hoot's right name was Walter, but no one ever called him that. He was awfully nice to me on that trip.

Back in Baltimore after a fabulous seven days, I received a call from Richards to report to his office. "Brooks," he told me, "we're going to send you down to York today. John Lancaster will drive you there. Good luck."

Although I was beginning to get homesick already, I could hardly wait for that forty-mile drive to be over so that I could get to playing baseball. It had been great spending that week with the Orioles, but when you're a spectator and not playing, time goes by slowly. It wouldn't be that way in York, I hoped.

Chapter 10

The drive from Baltimore to York seemed to take forever. That forty miles of highway was the crookedest I'd ever been on. But Lancaster almost kept me from worrying about our chances there as he filled me in on the club from his extensive background and told me about the manager, George Staller, now our first base coach with the Orioles.

We drove straight to the park. When Lancaster introduced me to Staller, I felt like I already knew him. "Happy to meet you, Robinson," was his greeting. "Tomorrow night we'll play you at second base."

That was fine with me. Just play me, I begged silently. Although I felt third was my position, I was aware that Baltimore had seen me almost exclusively at second in Legion ball.

At that time York was in the center of a hotbed of minor league baseball. Its rivalry with the next town to the east—Lancaster—was torrid. No more than thirty miles separate the two, and their history goes all the way back to early colonial days and beyond, with Lancaster being known as the Red Rose City and York as the White Rose City. In fact, our team was nicknamed the White Roses, as the letters across the front of our uniforms plainly showed.

Though not a very big city in terms of area, York probably had a population of 40,000 or so when I played there. Streets in the city, which are laid out around a bend of Codorus Creek, have such names as King, Queen, Duke, Princess, and George. Like the English York, this Pennsylvania namesake has a great place also in the annals of its own nation.

Its baseball history now is just that—history. There's no longer a team in York but the Orioles draw real well from there. In fact, a fellow named George Trout who is an avid Baltimore fan comes down every year on York night and pins those stickum white roses on every one of the Orioles. To this day Billy Hunter, one of our coaches, wears one right on the beak of the oriole on his hat.

Back in 1955, the Piedmont League was big. York was the Orioles' number one Class B farm club and the place they sent all the very young prospects. I never did know if they really felt I could play B ball, but that's where they sent me and I stuck.

I've always felt particularly fortunate in being sent to York because of the opportunity of working under Staller, a super guy, and a great manager to play for as a first year player.

The job of a minor league manager is one I don't envy, especially in the lower leagues where there are a lot of teenage youngsters—like me back in 1955—to contend with. The minor league manager is everything. He's the manager, the coach, the teacher, the bus driver, the trainer, the clubhouse custodian. But, most time-consuming, he's father, in fact, literally father-confessor, to all his players.

George had to deal with everything from the homesickness of a kid like me to the problems of some young married guy who couldn't afford to bring his wife to York and had all kinds of domestic difficulties. If ever a day went by when Staller didn't have to handle some personal crisis for one of the players, I'd be surprised.

But George was a master at it. He seemed always to have the answer. I know he did in the hours he spent being a nursemaid to Brooks Robinson, a boy away from home for the first time. Probably he spent as much time that way as he did coaching me on the field.

Second base, although I had played it more of my American Legion career than third, was still a problem for me on the field. I needed improvement handling the pivot on the double play. In addition, I just didn't have the range either way to be a solid second baseman. Nevertheless, about the first fifty games I played for York were at that position.

Staller still kids me about those days. "I saw you make a double play one time," he reminisced recently, "and I said to myself, 'I've got to get him out of there. He's gonna get killed.' "

I don't know if that's true or not. I do remember, however, the night George called and said, "Brooks, we think you're a third baseman. That's where we're playing you starting tomorrow."

For the rest of the season and for probably 99.9 percent of my baseball career that's where I've been. Though I've occasionally played at second or at short for Baltimore, I'm definitely out of position and hardly what you'd call of major league caliber at either place, not because I can't handle the glove work but because my speed just doesn't give me the necessary range and maneuverability.

That first year at York was a great one for me. Arriving after graduation in June, I missed a month and a half of the season but played all the rest of their 95-game schedule. The .331 which I hit was wonderful for someone just off the Little Rock Legion team, but most important to me was the fact that I hit with authority and a good bit of power. I had 117 hits in 354 times at bat, drove in 67 runs, and had 17 doubles, 3 triples, and 11 home runs—a high for me for the next five years. You'll appreciate my concern about my range when you look in the Baltimore brochure.* You'll find that Brooks Robinson stole one base that first year with York. It wasn't until 1959 that I raised that figure to two.

No one will ever call me a threat when I'm on base. Unless the guy in the batter's box hits the ball, my steals aren't even a minimal possibility. Three in one season is my all-time high, and there were two or three years when I didn't steal a base.

No matter how hard I look for the steal sign, it's never there for me. When Hank Bauer was manager of the Orioles in 1966, Luis Aparicio had his permission to steal on his own, without a sign. One day I asked Bauer, "Why don't you put me on my own to steal?"

"Okay," he agreed, "you can be on your own. But if you ever get thrown out it's going to cost you fifty dollars."

---

* See Appendix, p. 199.

[69]

Needless to say, I didn't take that kind of risk very often.

That first year in baseball, when you're doing everything you can to impress the club, is one you never forget. There was one particularly memorable day, however. It came somewhere about the middle of the season, on an off-day for us and Baltimore too, when they bused up to play us in York.

That game is still vivid in my memory. Here I was, only weeks out of high school, with only Class B experience and four years of Legion ball, getting ready to go against a major league club.

Paul Richards started Joe Coleman, Sr., a big right-hander with a lot on the ball. He had been Baltimore's most valuable player the year before, and I'll never forget my first look at him. It was in the opening inning and there were two men on when I came to bat. I don't recall the count, but the pitch was a fast ball, a little high and outside. I drove it deep over the left field fence for a home run. We went on to win that exhibition, 13–1, in one of my best nights at bat all year.

On the bench during the game some of the guys suggested that I might be changing my colors and leaving with Baltimore because I'd had such a good night. But instead they took Bob Hale, and, as we were living it up in that little York clubhouse, Bob kidded me. "Hey, slugger," he yelled so everyone including Paul Richards next door could hear it, "maybe you're the one they ought to be calling up."

Baltimore was loaded with young prospects. In a hurry to find young players who could do the job, Richards was moving them about like chessmen. Wayne Causey, who got about $35,000 to sign, was along with the Orioles but not playing much. We exchanged gibes with one another around the batting cage before the game. There was no rule about fraternization then, and besides, it was all in the family; Baltimore owned us all.

"When they call you up," Causey told me, "I'll buy the dinner the first night."

"You should," I shot back at him, "with all that money you got for signing."

It was kind of nice to see someone from the Southwest. No doubt about it, I was homesick for Little Rock, and especially the comfort and counsel of my dad.

Soon after that game Dad wrote that he was coming up to see me play. He said he'd fly to Baltimore and then take the bus to York. Rather than have me sit around waiting, since he didn't know the bus schedule, he planned to go to a hotel and then reach me at the place where I roomed with Gene Oden, one of our outfielders.

As nearly as we could calculate, Dad would be in late that night, so Gene suggested that we go to a movie to kill some time. I was a little concerned about not being home if Dad called, but Gene convinced me that in York—which wasn't that big—Dad wouldn't have much trouble finding me.

When we came out of the theater that night and started back to our house, it was several moments before I saw Dad on the other side of the street walking toward the hotel. Running across the street to greet him was one of the most emotional moments of my life. I guess at that instant, maybe more than any other, I really appreciated my dad.

Dad hadn't checked into the hotel yet, so the three of us walked down there together. We were making plans to have dinner when Gene broke in, "Brooks, I've got a couple of things to do. You and your dad will want to talk so I'll see you at the house later."

Dad and I spent a long time at dinner talking about home, the Legion team, Gary, Mom, all our friends. Most of

[71]

all, though, we talked about my baseball life with York. I wasn't setting the world on fire at the time. I was getting by in the field but my hitting was in a real slump.

There was some fine pitching in the Piedmont League that year. I'd been up against most of the clubs by the time Dad arrived and my results were not good. Over at the Brooklyn Dodger farm club in Newport News, Virginia, they had two fellows with great arms—Stan Williams and Larry Sherry. Williams, a big, overpowering pitcher, broke Johnny Vander Meer's Piedmont League strike-out record that season. When you recall that Vander Meer is the only pitcher in major league history to pitch back-to-back no-hit, no-run games and that he did that back on June 11 and 15 in 1938, you realize that Williams's achievement in 1955 was something.

Williams and Sherry could really fire that ball in. For me they were nothing but trouble. Contrary to the way the outfield automatically shifted back almost to the wall for Bob Allison, an outfielder for Hagerstown—my arrival at the plate caused no change at all. I don't remember my average at that point in the season but it wasn't very good.

"Maybe you're trying to pull everything into left," Dad said.

"That's possible," I admitted. "Our manager, George Staller, has been trying to teach me to hit more to right field and move the ball around. When you're batting against pitchers like Williams and Sherry, they keep you loose up there."

Dad's advice was the same he had given me a hundred times from the first day I began to play. "Why don't you quit worrying about the pitcher and just go up there to meet the pitch? Hit it wherever it's pitched. Remember, there are only three men covering that big outfield so you have plenty of space to drop a fair ball."

Dad's first full day in town we were to play Portsmouth in a night game. I don't know if it was because he was there or not, but after dinner when we went to the park, I just felt more comfortable, especially at bat. Along about the seventh inning, the fact that we were trailing by a run was really beginning to worry me, and I wanted to do something to get us back in the game. We had gotten a runner on first when I came up, thanks to a walk from Jim Barnhardt, a real strong-armed right-hander. Though Barnhardt wasn't a Stan Williams or a Larry Sherry, he was awfully good and had given me a lot of trouble.

He was primarily a breaking ball pitcher and threw most of his fast balls just on the outside corner, mainly because that's where all the pitchers had been getting me out. Barnhardt's first pitch was a breaking ball outside, but too far, and the umpire called it a ball.

Barnhardt tried to cross me up a bit with his next pitch, coming inside and pretty tight with his fast ball. It was about shoulder high and out over the plate. I dug in for a good cut. When it hit my bat it had that deep, resonant sound every batter likes to hear. No pinger that was going to lead into a double play, it took off like a rifle shot. As I rounded first and caught a glimpse of it, there was no doubt that it was going out over the left field fence almost down the line.

"You'd better stick around a while," I told Dad after we'd won a 4–3 victory. "Your coming seemed to pep me up. That's the best I've felt at bat in a couple of weeks or more."

Dad, who had never flown before this trip, remained in

York for the rest of that home stand—probably three or four days in all. As I recall, the Portsmouth game opened a three- or four-game series. The improvement in my play was proof beyond question that I had been homesick and looking for a familiar face. Seeing Dad's was the very medicine I needed.

The Piedmont League was an exciting one. Not only did most of the major league clubs farm out their top young prospects there, but most of the cities in the league were located close together, making for a lot of rivalry, especially among the fans. In those days in the York-Lancaster series, feelings were so intense it was almost like a little World Series.

But when the Piedmont's season ended in early September and Paul Richards called me up to the Orioles, I was more than ready to go. As excited as I was, the ride there looked like a five-minute run down to the neighborhood store in York. Now it was the big show and my first shot at the majors—although I was doubtful that I'd do much more than occupy bench space.

11

John Lancaster turned up after our final game at York to take me to Baltimore the next morning. After I had dressed and collected my gear, I went in to see George Staller.

"I want to thank you for all you've done for me," I told George.

"I don't think you'll be coming back here," he said. "I think you're on your way to the major leagues to stay."

"If I am," I assured him, "I owe it all to you. Thanks again."

We left early the next morning since the Orioles had an afternoon game with the Senators at Memorial Stadium. Once in the city, we went directly to the park, where I lost no time checking out my Baltimore gear and getting dressed. I was in such a hurry to be out on the field that even though this was the first chance I might have to play in the majors, I didn't notice what number I wore that day.

After infield practice I was sitting on the bench waiting for things to get started when Luman Harris, who was coaching for Paul Richards, came up to me.

"Robinson, you're in there at third," he notified me. Just like that—no preliminaries, no advice, just, "You're in there."

Shocked, I hardly heard Luman tell me that Don Leppert, who had been playing third base, was not feeling well and couldn't play.

"Get your glove, Robbie," he was saying, "and get out there."

Here I was, the first day in the major leagues, practically the first hour, really, and suddenly I'm out there to play third against the Senators. Gus Triandos was playing first, and just about the time he fired a grounder over to me to field, the public address announcer broke in: "Playing third base in place of Don Leppert and batting sixth, Brooks Robinson."

I almost blew the throw back to Triandos. Suddenly, the full realization hit me. I'd graduated from Little Rock Central on May 28, 1955. Hardly four months later here I was playing third base for the Baltimore Orioles, and the lead-off man for the opposing team, Washington, was one of the greatest third basemen of the time, a star whose career I'd followed for years—Eddie Yost. To me he was the epitome in fielding third basemen even though everywhere you went in baseball you kept hearing the opinion that Pie Traynor was the greatest third baseman ever.

Eddie Lopat, a nifty little left-hander who'd spent almost eight years with some of the great New York Yankee teams under Casey Stengel, was starting for us. He'd come to

Baltimore about midseason. Watching him as he fired his final pitches before Yost came to bat, I was almost overcome thinking back to some of those great World Series games he'd been involved in when I was at Little Rock Central.

At this moment, however, Baltimore, under Richards, and Washington, under the late Charlie Dressen, were still locked in the battle they had been fighting all year to stay out of the cellar. The Orioles were currently on the bottom and battling to grab seventh place, which they ultimately did by the narrow margin of four games.

As nearly as I can remember, Freddie Marsh was playing second and Willie Miranda was at shortstop. Hal Smith, in his first season with the Orioles, was the catcher. Dave Philley was in left; Chuck Diering, who played a few games at third earlier in the season, was in center; and Cal Abrams, who'd broken in with the Dodgers back in the great Brooklyn days around 1949, was in right.

When my first at-bat came in the second inning, Chuck Stobbs, a rather thin left-hander who'd been quite a pitcher for the Red Sox before coming to the Senators, had no trouble with me. I was what you'd call an easy out in my first big league appearance.

We were leading 2–0 when my turn came around again in the fourth inning. Although Stobbs was trailing, his stuff looked awfully good to me, accustomed as I was to Piedmont League pitching.

Stobbs's first pitch was a curve ball that caught one of the corners for a strike. It made me realize that up here in the American League the pitchers could almost call the spot where the ball was going to come in over the plate. A change-up dipped a little low, and the third pitch was a fast ball, maybe a little inside. I took a good rip at it and laced it into short left field for a single—my first in the major leagues.

"Welcome to the major leagues," Mickey Vernon, the Washington first baseman, greeted me after I'd made my turn and come back to the bag.

As long as I can remember reading box scores, Mickey Vernon had been a star in the American League. In fact, when he first broke in with Washington in 1939, I was just two years old, and for me baseball meant waiting at the front window every day with my glove and cap for my dad to come home and play catch. Now in 1955, standing on first base in Baltimore Memorial Stadium beside Mickey Vernon after my first hit in the American League, I was the happiest guy in all of baseball.

My final at-bat came in the eighth inning. Triandos, who looked more like a football tackle than a first baseman and catcher, led off the inning with a slashing double down the left-field line. Richards wisely elected to put in Dave Pope, a utility outfielder who had pretty good speed, to run for Gus. Bob Hale, a pinch hitter who'd been with me at York, and Hal Smith both were outs. Now it was my turn.

Stobbs had been replaced by Webbo Clarke, a left-hander from Colon in the Panama Canal Zone. A fidgety kind of pitcher, Clarke moved around a lot. I wondered at the time if he wasn't almost as nervous as I was, although as a relief pitcher he'd been in a few more games. It was my first time up, however, with a runner in scoring position and Baltimore needing a base hit by me to score. We had only a one-run lead, 2–1, and we could surely use some insurance out there on the scoreboard in center field. Clarke's first pitch was a little low and maybe off the plate a bit, but I liked its looks. I drove the ball into the hole in left center for a single that scored Pope from second with the insurance run.

Standing on first base, I couldn't believe it—two for four in my first day in the major leagues. I really have no idea how astronauts feel orbiting in space, but at that moment I was up among the feathery clouds that were hovering over Memorial Stadium. All the guys, including Paul Richards and Luman Harris, came around to congratulate me in the clubhouse afterwards.

Bob Hale, who'd come up from York about midseason and had played quite a bit at first base when Triandos was catching, offered to pop for dinner that night. But before I could do anything, I had to get to the Southern Hotel, where Lancaster told me to check in after the game.

There was one thing even more important than that. Dropping my bags off at the desk and still not checking in, I made a bee-line for the phone booth to call the folks back in Little Rock. "Dad," I said, excitement brimming over in my voice, "they called me up today, and I just played my first game for the Orioles."

I didn't even give him much of a chance to say hello, great, wonderful, or anything as a deluge of words poured forth.

"I went two for four, knocked in a big run in the eighth inning, and I can't believe the whole thing."

By then Mom and Gary were at the phone too. Our conversation must have been wild because I remember looking out of the phone booth and seeing people staring back at me. No doubt my voice was so loud that I really didn't need that telephone.

"Dad," I exclaimed, "I don't know why I was playing in York all year. This is my cup of tea; this game up here is for me."

That was a great day, and a great start for a kid, but the remaining weeks of the 1955 season brought Brooks Robinson back to reality in a hurry. Dad had tried to warn me on the phone.

"That's a great beginning, Buddy," he agreed, "but it's only the beginning. Remember, there'll be days when you don't get a hit. Be prepared for those days."

I needed to be, because they arrived in a hurry. I played the rest of the season, almost every game, at third base. By the time it was over, I found I had gone 0 for 18 after that first game and had struck out 10 of the 18 times. The two hits I got that first day were all I had in my 22 at-bats in 1955.

Those American League pitchers made me look like just what I was—a young, green, immature eighteen-year-old who'd been lucky that first day against Washington. They all made me look bad. The breaking balls they threw had me reaching out just like I did when I was a kid knocking rocks out into the woods with a broom handle. When they threw me those soft, blobby changes, I went after them as if I was digging into the candy jar but coming up empty.

One pitcher made me look the worst of all. That was Frank Sullivan, a Californian who looked more like he belonged in pro basketball playing center than pitching for the Red Sox. Close to six-seven and well over two hundred pounds, he had that big, easy motion that seems characteristic of products from the West Coast.

Sully was all arms, and that ball seemed to come out of his elbow, his shirt sleeve, or some other hidden place. I fanned nothing but air with him. He must have struck me out three or four times. Looking back over his record now, I can understand why. That was Frank's best year in the majors. He won eighteen and lost thirteen with an earned run average of 2.91. The most impressive statistic, however, was his 129 strikeouts in 260 innings, and Brooks Robinson contributed three or four to that count.

That man, more than any of the others in those few games, brought me to the realization that the pitchers were so far ahead of me that if I was ever going to make it and stay in the big leagues, I'd really have to work hard to improve my hitting.

Some years later, after I'd established myself in the major leagues, I reminisced with some of the guys about those first few games. I was embarrassed even then to think how bad I must have looked when pitchers like Frank Sullivan just knocked the bat right out of my hands.

"There was a really big question," one of them admitted, "whether Brooks Robinson could hit big league pitching."

Chapter 12

On the flight back to Little Rock after the close of the season, I reviewed in my mind what had happened to me since walking off the graduation platform at Little Rock Central High with my diploma and a set of dreams about being a big league baseball player.

I'd gotten the contract I was so concerned about, had done quite well in a pretty good minor league with York, hitting .331. I'd even made the Baltimore batting order at eighteen. But I'd also discovered that those pitchers in the American League had guns in their hands rather than baseballs.

There were a couple of other important matters on my mind as we flew west. For one thing, I needed a car, no matter where I played next year. It just didn't work bumming rides with other people. With no car, I was limited to doing what they wanted, regardless of my preferences. Then also, I had more than just casual concern after going 0 for 18 as to whether I was going to be able to handle that major league pitching.

If I didn't come around and do better next year, whether with Baltimore or the next higher farm club than York, I might find myself in the same unfortunate situation with so many young guys who fail to make it in baseball.

"He's a good field, no-hit prospect," is a tag you hear constantly in baseball. I didn't want to be stuck with it. But if that was to be my label then I'd better be prepared for some alternatives. As we approached Little Rock, I'd made two important decisions. I'd wait to see where I was sent for the 1956 season before deciding to buy any car, and I would definitely enroll in college.

My homecoming was far more joyous than my departure on Memorial Day. It seemed like a year since then, though it was actually only a little less than four months. During that time, I'd grown a lot in almost every respect. I knew how to move around the country on my own, take care of myself and my personal needs, and guard my money so it would cover my expenses from one pay check to the next. In fact, I even saved a little.

But my plans to enroll at Little Rock Junior College all ended more quickly than they had started when Baltimore decided it would be better for me to get more experience by playing winter ball in South America. Because I'd not started the season until after graduation, I'd played only 95 games of York's 140-game schedule. I could see that it was for my benefit to agree.

They sent me to Barranquilla in Colombia where I played for the Willard Battery Company team. Thirteen of us young Orioles, all single, lived in a huge house with six or seven bedrooms which was provided by the Willard people. In our fifty or sixty games against three other teams in the area, I found the level of competition a little higher than York. Certainly it seemed good enough to enable me to gain the experience I'd lost by not being with York from the start of the season in April. And I hoped it would speed me along toward the big leagues.

After the winter season in Barranquilla, I could look ahead to February and spring training with the Orioles in Scottsdale, Arizona. Getting word from Paul Richards to join all the Orioles at the major league camp was reassuring. I had been afraid I might have to report to the minor league camp at Dunedin, Florida. My memory of those few games in September with Baltimore and that 2 for 22 and .091 batting average was still quite vivid.

When the folks took me to the airport to catch the plane to Phoenix, Dad gave me one parting bit of counsel. "Don't press too hard," he advised me, "and don't take it too hard if they send you back down to the minor leagues. We hope it will be San Antonio because that's not too far to drive to see you play."

Never having been to a training camp, I couldn't believe we were going to be living in such a glamorous setting as the plush Camelback Inn. Scottsdale in February has a wonderful climate and is an ideal place to get in shape. But we paid a price for all our luxury. That first week, I discovered why some of the veterans called Paul Richards a tyrant. He really worked us hard but I always felt he was fair.

Although you always dream the impossible dream—in my case sticking with the Orioles all year—I was not surprised after a week or so when Richards called me into his office. We'd had a really tough workout that day under the broiling Arizona sun. "Brooks," he told me, "we're going to send you down to our Double A Texas League club at San Antonio. That's a big jump from York, but we think you can handle it."

Much to my surprise, I wasn't at all disappointed about being sent down. I think I knew it had to come. I just wasn't ready, with my nineteenth birthday still more than three months away, to play in the major leagues—even with Baltimore, where the emphasis was on youth and re-building. And the pitching in the American League obviously was still too much for me.

The next morning, John Lancaster handed me my ticket and travel money. Then he drove me over to Phoenix and the airport—the first leg toward Dunedin and the Orioles' minor league camp. Before I got on the plane to Miami, I called home to tell the folks what had happened. I wanted to let them know where I'd be staying in Dunedin and, as time permitted, to share some of the details Lancaster had given me about the club I'd been assigned to.

John filled me in again on my new field manager, of course—a fellow named Joe Schultz. His briefing included all the obvious details, such as Joe's having been a former major league catcher with the old St. Louis Browns before they were transferred and became the Baltimore Orioles. I learned later on that Joe's father was Germany Schultz, a famous major league player in the early 1900s who could play almost every position. Baseball was literally bred into Joe Schultz, and those of us with the San Antonio Missions in 1956 will remember him forever.

There was some really fine young talent on the club, including my old roommate from York, Gene Oden. Bobby Adams, who'd played for several years in the majors, mostly with the Cincinnati Reds, was a seasoned major league second baseman, and we had a solid first baseman in Fritz Marolewski. In the outfield Carl Powis and Stan Hollmig were good power hitters.

I'd split the season in York between second and third. No one in Scottsdale had said anything to indicate I'd be anywhere but at second with the Missions, but the obvious presence of Bobby Adams with all his experience left a definite question in my mind as the plane winged toward Florida.

Within the hour of my checking in at Dunedin, Schultz came up to me. "Arky," he said, "you're playing third base for us, so get your glove and get out there."

There wasn't even a formal introduction from the brusque, sharp-speaking Schultz. But Lancaster had told me not to worry about his bark because he didn't bite. Joe's voice didn't match the man. It was high and shrill, and no matter how many people were in the park or how loud they yelled, you could always hear Schultz screaming out directions on the field.

After the first day's workout in Dunedin, I was in the clubhouse drinking a Coke and eating an ice cream bar when Joe came up. "Arky," he remarked, "I want to tell you one thing. You can't get to the big leagues eating ice cream and drinking sody pop."

That's the first time he had seen me eat a thing but that didn't matter. From then on he needled me almost every day about "ice cream and sody pop."

He never changed what he called me either. Schultz had played his early years with Pittsburgh in the National League when Arky Vaughn was the Pirates' shortstop, so anyone from Arkansas, as far as Schultz was concerned, was automatically Arky—including me. He was the first and only one to call me that. Rarely during that entire season with San Antonio did he say Robinson, and never, so far as I can remember, did he call me Brooks. It was ironic that although Vaughn had been born in Clifty, Arkansas, he had actually spent most of his life in California. But that didn't matter. To Schultz both of us were Arky.

After we broke camp in Florida, we played our way west to San Antonio. Even though it was April, the Texas weather was warm and most of our games were at night. I got off to a horrible start, but Joe stuck with me all the way and I played every one of the 154 games for the Missions. There were times, however, when I felt sure I was going to be benched and shipped back to York or some other minor league affiliate. Fortunately, my work in the field at third, where I hadn't played much for years, rapidly came around.

After going hitless one night against Billy Muffett of Houston, a right-hander who later played with the Cardinals, I went to Schultz for help the next day.

"Can you pitch some extra batting practice to me tomorrow?" I asked Joe.

"Be at the park at ten tomorrow morning, Arky," he acquiesced, "and we'll work on it."

For more than an hour the next day, Joe pitched to me. But after the first few minutes, he stopped, walked off the mound, and came down to talk to me. "You've got to learn to go with the pitch," he insisted. "You're trying to drive every pitch out of the park. You're not a power hitter. You've got to move the ball around, go where it's pitched."

Then he took the bat and showed me a more controlled swing. And he showed me how to move my feet around so I could hit to right field.

"You're not a home run hitter," he declared. "Now,

[87]

Arky, forget about being a home-run hitter. Just try to hit the ball hard. Go for singles. If you'll do that, you'll get your share of home runs, but they'll be natural home runs."

Joe went back on the mound and resumed pitching to me. Suddenly, I began to get the feel of hitting with the pitch and hitting sharply. It was more than an hour and my hands were really hurting from the sting of hitting a hundred or so baseballs before Schultz called it quits.

That was one of the most productive batting practice sessions I ever had. For the first time, I was able to do with the bat what coaches and managers had been telling me to do for years.

Things didn't instantly turn around. The three digits representing my average were still down closer to those of my weight than I liked. But I had the feeling things were beginning to come together.

It was further tonic for my improving state of mind to get home from the park one night and find a letter from Dad. I'd talked to him a couple weeks before about a car. It looked as if I was going to stick with San Antonio, and in those Texas cities, nothing is measured in blocks; it's always miles.

"Dear Buddy," Dad wrote. "I've bought that Buick Special you wanted. I thought I might drive down to San Antonio next week and deliver it to you."

That was the kind of a message I needed. Dad always seemed to inspire me, something I would certainly be happy to have happen. I was almost nineteen and although my average had crept back up to around .240, I was still not pleased with my performance.

According to our schedule, we'd be home for a few days for a very important series with Fort Worth, then a strong

Dodger farm club. They had a lot of power from Jim Gentile, another of those king-sized first basemen like Gus Triandos, and an equally tall but much slimmer outfielder named Don Demeter. Both later played with the Dodgers and Gentile had some outstanding years with Baltimore in addition. Demeter quite successfully stayed around the majors for eleven years.

The Dodgers, as Fort Worth called their club, and Dad showed up almost at the same moment. I don't know which made me happier—the maroon 1956 Buick Special or my performance at the plate during our series with Fort Worth.

The first game, Dad was in the stands along with a friend from Little Rock—V. L. Washburn, a detective who lived next door—who had helped him drive the five hundred and some miles to San Antonio. Coming up in the eighth with a man on second and the game tied, 1–1, I slashed a single over Dick Tracewski's head that gave us a 2–1 win. The next game we took Fort Worth apart, 8–3, my contribution being a home run and a double. Now my bat was really helping the club. And it continued to do so in the third game, as I got two singles into right field. We swept the series, and it gave my morale a tremendous boost to have had such an important part in our triumph.

When Dad got on the train to go back to Little Rock, I was sorry to see him leave. Even though this was my second season away from home and San Antonio was a lot closer than York, I was homesick.

"Whenever you come," I wanted Dad to know, "I seem to snap out of my slump." This has been true all through my career—just why I've never been able to figure out. When the folks are around I guess I just want to do my very best.

As the Texas League season moved along, my batting average picked up bit by bit. Late in the season when we were playing at Shreveport on a hot, humid Louisiana night after a lot of rain, I got a deep single into right center that almost got away from the outfielder. As I turned first, I decided to try for second. Coming into the bag, I could see the throw, but as I started my slide, I seemed to get hung up in the wet dirt. My spikes caught a bit and something went pop in my right knee.

It was hardly what you would call a picture slide. In fact, it was downright awkward. When I tried to get up the pain was terrible. Schultz beat the trainer to second base. After a quick examination, the trainer gave me news I didn't want to hear. "It looks like a torn cartilage. I can't tell how bad. We'll have to wait a day or two to see."

By the next morning, the knee was balloon size. I could hardly walk. Driving was next to impossible. But after two or three days of therapy, heat, whirlpool baths, and massage, I was able to start running and was back in the lineup in less than a week. Still, the knee bothered me off and on throughout the season, especially when I tried to make quick starts while running the bases.

Even with the knee, it was a good year. Though my batting average of .272 was considerably below the .331 I hit at York, it has to be remembered that Texas League pitching was much better than that in the Piedmont. I hit nine home runs and drove in 74 runs while leading the league in defense at third base with a .959 fielding average and 213 put-outs—not a bad record for a nineteen-year-old.

As I drove the Buick Special back toward Little Rock it was with new confidence for the future.

The winter between seasons seemed like forever. I went
to Little Rock Junior College for classes, spent a lot of
time working out playing basketball, and did some running
and extensive therapy work on that bothersome knee. But
October eventually gave way to Thanksgiving and then
Christmas and when, after all the New Year's Day football
games, I began heavy workouts to be ready for spring
training, the knee seemed to improve.

When I told the folks good-by at the Little Rock airport, it was with the strong belief that I'd be the Baltimore
third baseman. Even the knowledge that during the middle
of the 1956 season Paul Richards had acquired one of the
great third basemen of all time—George Kell of the Chicago White Sox—didn't squelch my optimism. Reading
about the trade in San Antonio had made me a little de-

spondent at the time, until Joe Schultz convinced me that Kell was just a stopgap measure and that I was the third baseman of the future.

Schultz's estimate of the situation had been amply confirmed when after the close of the Texas League season Richards used me to play all thirty-three games at third. I hit .227 and got my first major league home run one afternoon against Washington.

So I was really charged up as we had our family goodbys and I headed west once more for Scottsdale and the warm Arizona weather. Paul Richards's words after the close of the 1956 season in Baltimore were still ringing in my ears. "Brooks, you're a fine prospect, one of the best I've seen in years."

His instructions to me to go home, stay in good shape and work on strengthening my knee I'd followed to the letter. I could hardly wait to get out on that field in Scottsdale.

The most important thing happened the first day of spring training. Richards turned me over to Kell to work on everything about my game at third base. I couldn't have had a finer teacher. Kell, who had been around baseball fourteen years, was a thorough master not only of technique but all the little secrets that come of long experience. Few men could hit with more authority and regularity. Nine times he had hit over .300, and in 1949 he had led the American League in hitting with a .343 average, tying one of the greatest hitters of all time, Ted Williams of the Red Sox. George ultimately won the batting title by a hundredth of a point.

Kell worked with me hour after hour—not so much with my fielding, where he was satisfied that experience was mainly what I needed, but on my batting. "You've got to

[92]

develop better control of your bat," he insisted in our innumerable talks. "Don't be a free swinger trying to take it out of the park. Be sure you get a piece of every ball you take a cut at. That way you will reduce your strike-outs." That was an area I knew I had to work on. I had struck out sixty-four times my first year at York and another fifty-seven at San Antonio, not counting ten that first year at Baltimore in 1955.

As we left Arizona and headed east, Richards's words were like a serenade: "Brooks, you're my third baseman."

That was the greatest thing I'd heard. Now all those dreams were possible if I could just play the way I had to. Kell assured me I'd have no problem in the field, that Paul would keep me in the line-up if I kept my bat controlled and cut down on my strike-outs. Then Kell, as player-coach, would alternate on first base with Bob Boyd, a streaky line-drive hitter the Orioles had acquired for the 1956 season from the White Sox.

Opening at third base for the Birds, I'd just gotten off to a good start when disaster struck. About ten or fifteen games into the season, in a game with the Senators, Lyle Luttrell, who played briefly for Washington at short that year, picked up a pretty well-hit grounder of mine. His throw to first was low, almost in the dirt, and right along the baseline. As Mickey Vernon dug out the ball, I realized he was going to have to hand-tag me to make the put-out. But in my cut to avoid the tag, my left leg abruptly crumpled under me with a terrible pop, and the pain was almost unbearable. I didn't need anyone to tell me what had happened. Richards, Kell, and the trainer were on the field immediately and Pete Runnells, playing at third for the Senators that day, told me to lie still.

Dr. Erwin Mayer was in the clubhouse when they brought

me in on a stretcher. It was the same knee I had hurt that wet, rainy day the year before at Shreveport, and it was locked. If I tried to move it, waves of pain swept over me. "The cartilage is torn all the way," was Dr. Mayer's verdict. "We'll have to operate."

Dr. Edmond McDonnell, a most able orthopedic specialist, did the actual surgery. I was hospitalized for about ten days, after which I gimped around the clubhouse the next three or four weeks while the Orioles were home. Once the heavy bandage was removed and I began therapy, my recovery came fast—undoubtedly spurred on by the good job Kell and Billy Goodman were doing alternating at third while I was out of action. Both were hitting around .300, and Baltimore, now making its move under Richards, no longer was buried in a fight with Washington to stay out of the cellar.

Two months to the day when he had operated, Dr. McDonnell gave me the okay to go back to full-time playing. I was running in the outfield getting my wind back and trying to recover my stamina when Paul Richards called to me.

"Brooks," Richards began—and I knew what was coming next—"we're going to send you back down to San Antonio. We want you to get down there with Joe in the warm weather and play your way back into shape."

A lot of my dream castles collapsed right then. Though I had really known this had to come, I hadn't wanted to admit it, even to myself. Being aware of the possibility doesn't make it any easier, either. All my dreams of being a major league ball player seemed to vanish with those few words. But Paul assured me that as soon as my knee was back to full strength and I was in shape, he'd call me back up.

Having signed me to a major league contract, Baltimore had only three options on me. They had already used two —the first when they sent me to York my first year and the second when they sent me to San Antonio in 1956. But at this particular time in the American League, if a player was sent down and brought back before thirty days, the option was not lost.

Once more it was pack up and move out. Convinced by George Kell that I'd be back in two or three weeks, I decided to leave the Buick Special in Baltimore and fly to San Antonio. George advised me to do a lot of running every day, lift weights, and maintain the heavy therapy program Dr. McDonnell planned for me.

When I arrived at the Mission clubhouse, Joe Schultz was the first person I met. "Okay, Arky," he greeted me, "they sent you down here to get back in shape, so you'd better be ready because I'm going to be all over you."

That was Joe's way of saying hello.

The next month, playing in 33 games, I hit .266. Most important, I struck out only 16 times in 124 at-bats. Schultz ran me ragged. And when he didn't have me running in the outfield, he'd get the fungo bat during batting practice and chase me back and forth on third base. Within two weeks, I was ready. Dr. McDonnell had done such a great job of repair that my knee didn't bother me a bit.

We were dressing in Tulsa one night to play the Oilers when Harry Brecheen, one of Richards's coaches, came in the door. Seeing Harry always took me back to my school-boy days and the old Philco radio in the front room where I had listened so often to the St. Louis Cardinals games in which he had starred as pitcher. "Harry 'the Cat' Brecheen," read the bubble gum card on him in my scrapbook, "15-game winner for World Series champion St. Louis in 1946." After I signed with Baltimore, I used to kid Harry about being the only major leaguer ever born in Broken Bow, Oklahoma.

He made a bee-line toward my locker when he got in the clubhouse. "Brooks," he demanded, "how's the knee?"

I knew then that Richards had sent him down to take a look at me. "It's better than ever," I assured him. "I'm ready to go back."

Brecheen, a little, broken-arm left-hander, spent a dozen years in the majors, all but one with St. Louis. The fact that he changed uniforms and joined the Browns in his final season must account for his ending up with the Baltimore organization, because in 1954, the year after he retired, the Browns moved and became the Orioles.

Harry watched the entire Tulsa series and then followed us on to Oklahoma City. About the second game of the series—and I think the day before the thirty-day grace period ended—Harry came in the clubhouse after the game. I'd had a good night at the plate, getting two hits to help us win the game.

"Pack your gear, Brooks." Harry's words were the sweetest ones I'd heard in a long time. "We're going back to Baltimore right away."

Hurriedly arranging with my roommates, Bob Schmidt and Dick Ludke, to pack the rest of my clothes and ship them to me when the club got back to San Antonio, I stowed my baseball gear in a Missions road bag and bundled up my bats as well.

Then I stopped in to see Schultz, one of the great men in a young baseball player's life. With his feet up on the desk and wearing only his shorts, Schultz gave me the word. "Nothing personal, Arky, but I don't want to see you down

[96]

here again. Stay up there this time. Remember," he cautioned, as Brecheen came in to hurry me along, "go with the pitch and your average will pick up."

Richards had been splitting third base up among Kell, Jim Brideweser, and Wayne Causey, the bonus baby from Louisiana. Not much of the 1957 season remained when we arrived in Baltimore but what there was I finished out on third. All told, counting the games before I tore my knee apart, I played in 50 games that year, hit .239, drove in 14 runs and got a pair of home runs. The thing that pleased me most, however, was that I struck out only 10 times in 117 at-bats. And quite a few of those strike-outs were in the first half of my split season.

All the patience and work of Kell and Joe Schultz definitely improved my batting, particularly my ability to go with the pitch and to get at least a piece of a lot of balls I swung at. But Richards was still not satisfied.

Determined to change things around at Baltimore, he'd had players coming and going almost on a daily basis as long as trades were permitted, and he'd jumped the club from near last in 1957 to fifth place, only 21 games behind the champion Yankees. The club had played .500 ball and was only a game out of fourth place.

A few days before we packed it in for the season, Richards called me into his office in the clubhouse. "Brooks, we're pleased with your progress." His words were precise. "But we think you need a lot more work, especially after missing two months of the season because of your knee surgery. We want you to go to Cuba and play winter ball."

That was fine with me. I knew I needed more work after sitting out those sixty days, and getting it in those surroundings would provide not only rigorous but pleasant therapy. The best winter league in baseball, Cuba's four clubs had a reputation for stiff competition, and Baltimore sent quite a contingent, as did the other major league clubs. Cinefuegos, the team I played for, had Pedro Ramos and Camillo Pasqual on the pitching staff; Dick Gray of the Dodgers had already been signed to play third so I was asked to play second; Pancho Herrera played first and Chico Hernandez short.

By the time that 1957 winter season was over I had to agree that I was back in tiptop condition, the kind of shape I'd been in early the previous spring. As I flew out of Little Rock in February for Scottsdale and spring training, all I could think about was staying with Baltimore all of 1958.

Above: When Brooks Robinson, Jr. was born May 18, 1937, this big white house at 106 Denison Street in Little Rock, Arkansas, was home. *Right:* 28-months-old Buddy, as his family called him, ready for a baseball practice session with his dad.

Left: Brooks Robinson, Jr., age 9, with Brooks Robinson, Sr. *Right:* 15-year-old Brooks in American Legion ball club uniform. Scene is back yard of Lloyd Court home where Brooks learned to hit rocks into woods with broom-handle bat.

Top left: Brooks Robinson scores field goal for Little Rock Central against El Dorado during 1954–55 basketball season. *Top right:* Working out at guard position, where Brooks won All-Big-Seven and All-State honors during his high school career. *Below, left:* Ready for some evening glove work at nearby field, Spring 1955. *Lower right:* High school graduate Brooks Robinson. Only two days following graduation ceremonies, Brooks, with his parents, signed contract with Baltimore Orioles organization.

Top left: Connie and Brooks Robinson in wedding portrait taken outside Christ the King Church in Windsor, Ontario, where they were married in October 1960. *Top right:* Toddler Brooks David Robinson at about age one with his parents at Father–Son game in Baltimore in 1962. *Left:* The Robinson clan in 1969. Brook's father holds granddaughter Diana while Grandmother Robinson (center), Brooks, Connie, and the boys look on.

Family day at Memorial Stadium, Baltimore, 1973: (left to right) Connie, Chris, Michael, Brooks David, Brooks, Diana. PHOTO BY TADDER/Baltimore.

George Kell (left), baseball's number one third baseman when Brooks Robinson arrived in the majors, coaches his most apt pupil. PHOTO BY JOE DI PAOLA.

Brooks Robinson holds dubious distinction of most beanings (7) suffered by one player in a major league career. Here he is carried from field after being hit in head by pitcher Ned Garver of the Kansas City Athletics on August 2, 1957. Brooks received mild concussion, required 10 stitches to close wound.

Baltimore's starting infield in 1960. Left to right: Ronnie Hansen, shortstop; Mary Breeding, second base; Walt Dropo, first base; Brooks Robinson, third base.

Robinson "twins," Frank and Brooks, after October 5, 1966, World Series game, during which each hit 1st-inning home runs off Don Drysdale for Orioles' 5–2 win. UPI telephoto.

Brooks (left) and Eddie Robinson (right) with Paul Richards, then Orioles' manager, hold autographed model Brooks Robinson bat. Brooks and Eddie for several years operated restaurant in Baltimore known as Gorsuch House, which now uses Brooks's name alone. PHOTO BY JAMES D. MCCARTHY.

Baltimore's 1964 infield. Left to right: Brooks Robinson, third base; Luis Aparicio, shortstop; Jerry Adair, second base; Jim Gentile, first base.

Brooks Robinson the younger
with the man who has been
the greatest single inspiration
to his baseball career—Brooks
Robinson the elder, his father.
PHOTO BY *Baltimore News-
American.*

Many consider Brooks Robinson (left) modern baseball's
greatest third baseman. Brooks
rates Clete Boyer (with New
York Yankees at time of this
picture) the greatest he has
ever seen. PHOTO BY JAMES D.
MCCARTHY.

Brooks has held the
legendary Harold "Pie"
Traynor in highest ad-
miration since boyhood.
Considered by most
baseball experts as the
greatest third baseman
of all time, Traynor
played for Pittsburgh
for 17 years.

Left: Brooks Robinson in classic stance, about to field ball during a game. Note new style glove with left index finger outside.

Above: Robinson grabs line drive hit by Cincinnati Reds' Johnny Bench to end first inning of Series game October 13, 1970. *Left:* Baltimore pitcher Mike Cuellar raises his arms in victory as he rushes to meet third baseman Brooks Robinson after Orioles' win October 15, 1970. Baltimore won Series in five games. WIDE WORLD PHOTOS.

At baseball's 1970 Awards Dinner. Left to right: Cincinnati's Johnny Bench, player of the year; Baltimore's Brooks Robinson, defensive player of the year; and St. Louis Cardinals' Bob Gibson, pitcher of the year. AP Wirephoto.

On tour in Vietnam in 1966. Brooks Robinson (second from left); Harmon Killebrew, Minnesota Twins' slugger (on Robinson's left); and Stan Musial (center, hatless), noted former outfielder of St. Louis Cardinals and now vice-president of that organization.

1972 American League All-Stars at Atlanta. Brooks Robinson is at far left. Others, left to right, are: outfielder Bobby Murcer, New York Yankees; outfielder Carl Yastrzemski, Boston Red Sox; first baseman Richie Allen, Chicago White Sox; manager Earl Weaver, Baltimore Orioles; catcher Bill Freehan, Detroit Tigers; shortstop Bobby Grich, Baltimore; second baseman Ron Carew, Minnesota Twins; outfielder Reggie Jackson, Oakland Athletics.

Chapter 14

Throughout the winter of 1957, Paul Richards was quoted repeatedly about the role young ball players were to play in the 1958 season. He had been emphasizing youth ever since he took over the Orioles in 1955. "Some day," he had told a writer then, "Baltimore will have a fine young team. When that happens, just observe ten seconds in memory of Paul Richards."

Several in the club, particularly George Kell, felt we were getting close to that stage. And I certainly wanted to be a central part of any youth movement by being the regular third baseman for Baltimore.

Richards had written and urged each of us to be in top shape when we arrived in camp because he wanted to get right down to work on fundamentals. He didn't want to lose anyone with blisters, pulled muscles, or any of the other ailments that develop if you don't do a lot of preparation before checking in.

Scottsdale was just what Richards warned. He worked us harder than I had ever worked in my life. By the end of each day I wasn't ready to do anything but eat dinner, watch a little television, and then hit the bed. Maybe some of the players in camp were able to go out on the town, but I wasn't among them.

Richards, a no-nonsense manager, wanted the most from his players, and he never hesitated to make his opinions clear. "I've been around a long time," he has stated more than once, "and I've had my fill of old players who put on a uniform just to go through the motions and then spend the rest of the night lapping up beer and telling how good they used to be."

Though quite a number of players, young and old, felt Richards was too tough, I never shared that conviction. Rather, it seemed to me that when he took the time to talk to any of us to correct an error or offer advice, he believed we could do what he was asking and we'd do well to try.

The improvement in playing skill from year to year made me feel most fortunate to have begun my career with Richards. There just aren't many men in baseball sounder than he, and certainly fewer put forth more effort to bring the best out of every individual player.

Paul was constantly correcting my batting style. He wanted me to stay close to the plate and hold the bat high —which I had done from the time I was old enough to play baseball—but he also wanted me to be selective about what I hit.

I wish I could also have been taught to be selective about what hit me. In all my earlier years in baseball, from grammar school on, I had never thought much about getting hit in the head. I'd been hit a lot, but never there. In fact, I'd never worn a helmet until I got to York. There we wore those small liners to protect us in the vital areas. I had always figured if you got hit in the head—well, it just didn't happen—all you had to do was duck.

But in winter ball down at Barranquilla with the Willard Battery team, I found out differently. Fortunately for me, they were testing a new type of helmet made of fiberglass and our manager made all of us wear them.

Earl Wilson, who later played for Boston and Detroit, hit me flush on the front of the helmet one night when he was pitching for Cola Ramon. The impact was so hard that the ball ricocheted right up and over the stands onto the street. He knocked me flat, sending my helmet sailing off to the backstop, and when I got up, there was a knot on my forehead as big as a golf ball.

Afterwards in the clubhouse, when we examined the helmet, we could see that the fiberglass was cracked and there was a baseball-sized dent in it which even bore the mark of the seams of the ball.

I'm told I hold the major league record for being hit in the head. Whether or not I do, the seven times I've been decked over the years is enough. That's the most dangerous part of baseball, and a record nobody would consciously go after.

The worst beaning I ever had was on August 2, 1957, in a game with Kansas City. Ned Garver, a pitcher with an assortment of pitches and great control, was on the mound. Although he had a reputation for working a batter first on one side of the plate and then the other, on this particular day he had pitched me one way—outside, outside, outside.

When a pitcher does that to you fairly consistently, you begin thinking outside and you begin to lean in a little more over the plate to keep your eye on the ball.

That's what I must have been doing when the next pitch from Garver came streaking in like a jet. I saw it coming but couldn't get out of the way. The ball slammed into the helmet just above my left eye, skidding up off the bill and crashing into the round part of the helmet. It shattered the helmet and I went down like a rock.

They rushed me to Union Memorial Hospital in Baltimore with a mild concussion. The doctors put ten stitches above my eye, and I spent two days in the hospital. When I was released, I had to sit out a few more days before getting back in the lineup.

My next tangles with the beanball—one in 1963 and the next in 1967—were not so serious, but reminder enough to evoke vivid memories of Garver's shot. One skimmed off the top of my helmet and another gave me a knot over my ear, with a headache thrown in for good measure.

By the time I had been nailed for a fifth knockdown— this one a blast right at the ear hole that kept my ear ringing for a week—I began to wonder if I had a blind spot, or if my reflexes were going on me. All kinds of thoughts like these kept going through my mind as they carried me into the dressing room. Again I stayed out a couple of days, but once back in the lineup, there was no time for such preoccupations.

I'm sure no pitcher intentionally tries to hit a batter. I read in the papers the next day after I'd been beaned the seventh time that Woody Fryman of Detroit came up to the plate and asked me how I was. That I don't remember —I was temporarily somewhere else.

Pitched baseballs come up to the plate doing about sixty,

seventy, or eighty miles per hour, depending upon who is throwing; and when a pitcher is trying to brush a batter back, a few inches can mean the difference. Pitchers who want to show the batter who's in charge are going to bust them in there from time to time. The batter had better be loose and agile or awfully quick moving his head.

I can't put it too strongly that *no one*—whether it be in Little League or the majors, in any kind of baseball— should ever go up to that plate to hit without a helmet and an earflap on. I would be scared to death without one.

Even after that first beaning in Colombian winter ball by Earl Wilson, when I began spring training in Scottsdale in 1958, it never dawned on me to stay a little looser at the plate or give a little ground in my normal stance. I just stuck my head out there and dug in. I was determined that my third year in baseball was all going to be spent in Baltimore with no stops in San Antonio or Vancouver.

By comparative standards that goal was realized, but it was not a season to boast about. My batting just wasn't major league standard, although my work in the field was very satisfactory. In many games I didn't get onto the field until the late innings when Richards would send me in for defensive purposes.

One day, toward the end of the season, and just when I needed it, Richards made a statement to the writers that really bolstered my spirits and made me more determined. "Some day," he said, "Brooks is going to help us at the plate just as much as he does with the glove."

In late September that year—September 20, 1958, to be exact—I'd been on the bench against the Yankees the whole game. Hoyt Wilhelm, remarkable in baseball history for pitching successfully in the majors on into his late forties, was working on a no-hitter when Richards put me in at third. In the ninth inning, Hank Bauer—who later on was to be my manager with the Orioles—came up to bat.

He was called Hammerin' Hank, and for good reason. He displayed pure power just walking from the on-deck circle to the batter's box. And when he stuck out that lantern-square jaw, tugged on the bill of his cap, and dug in, you'd better be ready if you were the third baseman because Bauer could tear your head off with a liner.

On this particular September day, there had been a drizzle falling off and on, and the field was slippery both on the grass and on the dirt. As Bauer dug in, I got in my usual crouch, leaning forward just a bit to have my body in motion to go wherever the ball was hit. Suddenly that big, blocky man dipped his bat forward, squared away, and put a perfect surprise bunt down the third base line.

Who ever would have thought that this hard-nosed ex-Marine gunner would employ that strategy to kill off Wilhelm's no-hit, no-run effort! I came charging in on the ball, trying hard not to lose my footing. At the same time, I was trying to catch a glimpse of where he was on the base path, for while he looked like a college tackle, Hank could run pretty well.

In a flash I realized that if I fielded the ball, there was no way I could throw Bauer out at first. As I watched, the ball began to bend to my right toward the foul line. I decided to let it roll, hoping it would go foul. My prayer was answered. The ball twisted into foul territory, where I grabbed it once it was clearly past the chalk line. Bauer, already on first, had to come back to the plate, and Hoyt had another shot at him. Wilhelm took care of things himself moments later when Bauer bounced one back to the mound and was thrown out.

There weren't too many bright spots in my 1958 season,

but being in on Wilhelm's no-hitter was the big one for me. It was the first no-hitter I had been involved in, but since the "old man" of the staff had done it—Wilhelm was thirty-six at the time—what is always a memorable triumph had special meaning for all of us on the club.

Chapter 15

As my first complete season of major league ball came to an end, I thought I was in pretty good shape. I soon found out differently.

Shortly before I was to leave Baltimore to drive back to Little Rock, Paul Richards decided this would be the best time for me to fulfill my military obligations. With my twenty-second birthday coming up in May, I might be called up at any moment by the Selective Service board.

The National Guard program in effect then—six months of active duty training with five and a half years of required duty time in the reserve—seemed to provide the simplest solution. So when I arrived back in Little Rock, I enlisted in the Arkansas National Guard.

From October 1958 until the following April, Brooks Robinson, Private, had plenty of opportunity to find out what real conditioning was. At Fort Chaffey, Arkansas, we marched, ran, drilled—day after day. And at Fort Hood in Killeen, Texas, it was no different. It only confirmed what I had discovered early on—that it's not possible to be a soldier and a third baseman at the same time. One thing had to suffer, and in this case, naturally, it was baseball. Although I played ball with others on the base whenever I could and, as spring arrived, even worked out with other professional players also on active duty—like Bob Weiss, a left-handed pitcher then in the Yankee organization, and Tony Asario, a second baseman—there were a lot of holes in my baseball skills when my six-month stint was up.

When I checked into camp in Miami, the Orioles' new location for spring training, there were only days left before we were to begin to play our way north for opening day in Baltimore. I was obviously miles behind everyone else. Although I felt super physically, my timing was terrible. My bat just wasn't doing what I wanted it to and even my fielding was not as sharp as I wanted it to be.

But again it was a remark by Richards to the press that assured me my situation was not entirely hopeless. Hugh Trader, a writer with the *Baltimore News-American,* inadvertently divulged Paul's comment when he told me about a chat he had had with Richards.

"If you're looking for a story," Richards had suggested to Trader, "why don't you write about the way Al Vincent [then an Oriole coach] hits fungoes? Look, he's been hitting ground balls to Robinson for an hour and hasn't missed yet. Wherever Robinson puts his glove, Vincent hits the ball right into it."

Richards, who seemed perfectly serious, had Trader believing him for a little while. "I'm telling you," Richards

[115]

declared to Trader after his little put-on was revealed, "that boy is going to become a star. A star. Remember that."

But even those words of praise weren't enough to restore my confidence completely when it became obvious that Billy Klaus had won the third-base job away from me. I kept telling myself it was because of my brief spring training and that I'd be right back at third in a short time. But there was still a question in my mind: was I good enough to be a major league third baseman?

The night before the opener, Klaus slipped in the bathtub and hurt his back. By the next morning he could scarcely move. When Richards told me I'd start at third, Billy's misfortune gave every appearance of being my good fortune. For the third year in a row, I was in the starting line-up for the Orioles' first game of the season.

My tenure was brief. I just didn't have it all together. My bat was entirely too slow for those American League pitchers who had a whole spring training season behind them, and I wasn't moving well in the field. During the first two or three weeks, I was in and out of the batting order. Paul would play Klaus or even use Jim Finigan, who had been acquired from the San Francisco Giants, at third more often than he did me.

By the time May rolled around, I was pretty despondent. I'd been to bat about twenty-five times, and my average was around .200, give or take a few points. The cut-down date was approaching, and it appeared, based on comparative playing times, that Paul would be going with either Klaus or Finigan at third and the other as the back-up man.

I hated to admit it even to myself. That meant there

wasn't room for a third man at third base and someone had to go down. Me?

We were in Chicago to play the White Sox when one morning Luman Harris, a coaching favorite of Richards, knocked on the door of my hotel room. "Brooks," he said when I opened the door, "Paul would like to have breakfast with you in the coffee shop."

His attempt to be casual didn't keep me from recognizing the message. I put on my tie and picked up my coat and key. Pretty sure what was going to take place, I experienced more than the usual feeling of having the bottom drop out of my stomach as the elevator descended to the lobby.

Richards was over in a corner alone, reading the paper and sipping coffee. "Sit down, Brooks," he motioned.

In those few seconds it takes to pull a chair out from a table and sit down, my life with the Orioles flashed by in instant replay.

I'd established myself quite solidly in 1958 at third base; I'd hit respectably at .238 and played in virtually every game, missing only nine, as I recall. It was not a sensational season, I'll admit. No one nominated me for rookie of the year, but I did get my feet on the ground, and 1959 looked to me like my big breakthrough.

Richards spoke with care. "Robbie," he said, "we've decided to send you down to Vancouver."

The world caved in on me, no doubt about it. Here it was just days away from my twenty-second birthday and I was getting a present like this—the word sending me down to the minor leagues.

Hanging my head in hopes that Paul wouldn't see the tears I knew were there, I tried to explain. "I reported late, you know, and didn't get to play too much. I thought

[117]

I would get more of a chance to play myself into shape after my National Guard duty."

Paul Richards was a most kind, consoling man in a situation like this. Having to tell you he was sending you down or dropping you from the batting order always seemed to bring out the father instinct in him. Contrary to the opinion of some over the years who have called him ruthless, I believe Paul Richards is a fair, honest, and considerate man who knows baseball and baseball players.

All kinds of thoughts were going through my mind. My fears that I'd reached the end of the line were realized. I wasn't of major league caliber. I'd been fortunate to play as much as I had. I was going down to the Pacific Coast League and I'd bounce around in the upper minors until one day there just wouldn't be a spot for Brooks Robinson.

Richards's next words brought me back to reality. "Brooks," he began again after what seemed like hours of quiet interrupted only by my fork scraping the scrambled eggs around, "you go down to Vancouver and play your way into shape. You need work. You'll be able to play every day for Charlie Metro, and if you show what I expect you to, I'll bring you back at the All-Star break. You're not going to get into shape here playing once or twice a week, and you're not ready to play every day for us."

There were still a lot of eggs on my plate and I hadn't touched my toast, but I couldn't finish them. Thanking Paul for breakfast, I got up from the table and went back to my room.

More than a few tears fell in my Chicago hotel room that morning as I carefully packed my clothes. Just about the time I had finished, the traveling secretary—good old John Lancaster—knocked on my door. "Don't worry, Brooks," he said, as he handed me my plane ticket, a bag with my baseball gear, and my travel money, "you'll be back real soon."

If I did more than nod it was a miracle.

When the airport bus stopped in front of the hotel, I was the first on. I took a seat in the last row on the street side so none of the guys would see me if they should come out of the hotel. It's a shattering experience to be sent down. Any ball player will tell you that. The younger you are the more difficult it is to accept.

At Midway Airport, I hardly remember boarding the plane. I know I did find a seat in the back by a window so I could look out and avoid conversation with anyone that might sit by me. I didn't want to have to go through that "where-are-you-going? what-do-you-do?" routine that happens so often on a plane.

"You go down to Vancouver and play your way into shape and I'll bring you back at the All-Star break." Paul Richards's words at breakfast kept coming back almost as if he were sitting beside me. Suddenly I realized the world hadn't come to an end, and I was glad I hadn't called home. At the time, of course, I didn't have the courage to tell Mom and Dad what had happened, but now I was beginning to see things in better perspective.

It was early evening when the plane landed in Vancouver. After gathering my luggage and my gear, I hopped in a cab and went directly to Capilano Stadium where the Vancouver Mounties played.

The first person I spotted as I walked in the clubhouse door was Wayne Causey.

"Brooks," he yelled, "what are you doing here?"

"They tell me you guys need some help," I retorted as we shook hands, "and they sent the best man to do the job."

Wayne laughed. Knowing full well how I felt, he maintained just the right degree of levity to keep me from feeling sorry for myself as he took me over to the manager's office to introduce me to Charlie Metro. "You'll start at third," Metro announced after a little chitchat about how things were in Baltimore.

Vancouver had a good club, and Charlie Metro was a fine manager. And we had a pretty good infield that first night, as I recall, with Buddy Barker on first; Marv Breeding, with whom I'd played winter ball in Colombia, at second; and Ronnie Hansen at shortstop.

It didn't take many games to convince me that Richards was right to send me down. I played myself into shape, had a terrific time, and what I thought was the biggest disaster in my young life proved to be one of the best things that ever happened to me. My fielding snapped back into shape, my swing was improving steadily, and my batting average hit a new high of .331 during my short stay.

Nevertheless, about a week or so after I arrived, things did turn dark. I'd hit a home run early in the game against Portland. In the fourth inning, with the field wet from a shower, a high, twisting fly ball that I was chasing off the third-base line kept drifting toward our dugout. Just as I stuck my glove up for the ball, I slipped. Trying to break my fall, I reached up with my right arm to grab onto a bar that would support me. But as I fell, my sweatshirt sleeve caught on a little hook on the guard rail atop the dugout and one of a series of those hooks ripped a jagged gash into my forearm.

The pain was excruciating. I screamed for someone to get me loose. All my body weight was on the hook and I could see the blood gushing out in spurts.

Charlie Metro was the first person to get to me. "It's going to hurt, Brooks," he warned. Then with some help from some of the other players, Charlie managed to release my arm.

The trainer slapped bandages around it and they rushed me to the hospital, where I was immediately taken into emergency surgery. As I lay on the table, my view of the gash was frightening. Now that pressure had stopped the bleeding, I could see everything that wicked-looking three- or four-inch-long tear exposed.

Gruesome as it may sound, it was beautiful to me to watch what happened when I moved my fingers. All the muscles and tendons moved too, including one major tendon which, if cut, would have meant extremely bad news for me.

"You're a lucky young man to have no permanent damage," the surgeon commented, when he had finished all twenty-two stitches of his sewing job. "If certain nerves and tendons had been damaged, it would have meant your career. As it is, I'm afraid you'll be out for the season."

The team went on the road right after that, leaving me behind in the apartment. They also left behind orders for dealing with those exposed hooks on the fence. The day after I got hung up on them, workmen were out there cutting them all off, taping over the ends, and covering them with foam rubber. I've often wondered how in the world they could have been left uncovered in the first place. Now when I see something potentially dangerous in a ball park, I don't just wonder about it; I tell someone.

As soon as the wound began to heal, I started doing exercises—careful ones so I wouldn't reopen it, but the kind that would help me heal properly. Within two weeks

I was hitting as well as I had at any time in my life, making a poor prophet of my doctor. I was really lucky the injury didn't maim me for life. Although the tendons are drawn a little, the condition never bothers me in any way now.

By the end of June I was having a great year, hitting up over .300 and providing Metro with a lot of help both at bat and in the field. Of course, I was also wondering which of 1959's two All-Star games would signal my return to Baltimore.

I got my answer just before the first one on July 7. When Charlie came to me and told me that the Orioles had sent for me, all my anguish of that early day in May was gone. I had turned everything around. My spirits were high. In retrospect that brief tour at Vancouver is one of the bright spots of my baseball career. In fact, I'll have to admit I was just a little unhappy about leaving Vancouver and the apartment I shared with Ronnie Hansen and Chuck Estrada.

As I prepared to fly back to Baltimore, my stat line was a pleasure to examine: in 42 games, I had averaged .331, scored 20 runs, made 54 hits—including 9 doubles, 2 triples and 6 home runs—driven in 30 runs, stolen two bases, and struck out only 14 times.

I picked the team up on the road—in Washington, as I remember—and was assigned to room with Jerry Walker, a young pitcher from Ada, Oklahoma. We hit it off real well, our already buoyant feelings having been further heightened by Jerry's winning the second game of a doubleheader on July 9, only two days after he had won the All-Star game in Los Angeles.

When we dined that night in a very elegant Washington restaurant, our hopes for Baltimore under Paul Richards were really soaring. We were moving up fast in the standings, and it looked as if we had a good chance at the pennant. As for me, now that I was back and on third base, there was no doubt that the world was my oyster.

Late in September, I went on the best batting tear of my young major league life, getting fifteen hits in thirty-two at-bats in a series of games ending with the Kansas City A's—an average of .469. In the final game of that series, Bud Daley, who always caused us trouble, was pitching for the A's. But this time we got to him early, grabbing a 4–0 lead for our pitcher, Jerry Walker, to work on, and things seemed to be under control.

By the seventh inning, Daley was gone and Murry Dickson, a little right-hander with some crazy stuff, was on the mound. He was all control, though with not much speed, and had a variety of off-speed pitches that could really distract a hitter.

After Walt Dropo had singled, it was my turn. Dickson gave me one of his better breaking pitches, but I was looking for it and drove it deep over the left field wall in the old Kansas City park. One of two home runs I hit in 1959, it made a great day for me.

As we headed toward our plane after the game, Richards walked along with me, and he seemed greatly pleased indeed. Things were looking up for Brooks Robinson.

Jubilation ran high as we boarded our special United Air Lines charter flight from Kansas City to Boston that hot, humid Missouri afternoon. Plodding up the ramp one step at a time behind Richards, I turned back every now and then to shout at somebody farther back in the line. I had just reached the ramp platform and ducked to enter the cabin door of the DC-6, when an unbelievably lovely vision stopped me dead in my tracks.

Smiling at me was this stunning, tall, slim, beautiful stewardess, her brown eyes flashing a smile of welcome that left me breathless. I just stood there as she showed Richards and some of the other players to their seats. When finally I was able to get myself in motion to follow her down the aisle, it was with the certain knowledge that this young lady was something else and that I had better try to do something about it.

To insure the chance of getting to talk with her, I dropped into the first available aisle seat. When Jerry Walker came on, I wouldn't budge.

"Move over, Brooks," he directed me.

"No, Jerry, I can't. I'll tell you why later."

Walker had to climb over my big frame with all his carry-on luggage and try to wiggle into his seat.

I was too busy trying to figure out how to get acquainted with this gorgeous creature who had just come into my life to have any sympathy for Jerry's plight. And anyway, I'm one of the lightest travelers of all. If I can't carry what I need in one three-suiter, then I don't take it.

As we waited to finish loading, I began to capitalize on the aisle seat I'd grabbed at Jerry's expense.

"Miss," I called, as the object of my attentions walked back toward the service deck. "Could you please bring me a glass of iced tea?"

Iced tea still happens to be my favorite cold beverage, and the wide, friendly smile this beautiful stewardess gave me when she said yes certainly enhanced my fondness for the drink that evening.

"Miss," I repeated the next time she came down the aisle carrying an empty tray of cups, "do you think I could have another iced tea?"

She had barely gotten the second glass to me when the captain's voice came over the intercom advising us to buckle our seat belts preparatory to take-off.

Once the "fasten-your-seat-belt" sign blinked off and everyone began to move around the plane, the stewardess came down the aisle yet another time to answer my light. I was holding my empty glass aloft.

"Don't tell me you want another iced tea," she said.

"I'm mighty thirsty, ma'am," I replied. "It's been a hot day in Kansas City, and iced tea really hits the spot."

By this time my confidence had been bolstered sufficiently to give me the nerve to do something I didn't have a great deal of experience at. As she walked back to the galley deck for the tea, I got up and followed her.

"I just want to tell you, miss," I said when I arrived in the tiny little galley, "I'm the only single guy on this ball club. All the rest are married. So, remember, if any of them try to talk to you—I'm the only single, eligible bachelor on the plane."

That wasn't exactly true. But at that point it was the only thing I could think of to try and isolate her from an army of guys who might be far more interesting to her than Brooks Robinson.

"Thank you," she said, gravely, handing me my third— or maybe it was my fourth—iced tea. "I'll remember that."

Fresh out of clever thoughts and appropriately charming words, I waved the iced tea glass to her in appreciation and headed back down the aisle. First I tried to read *Sports Illustrated,* then *Time.* Then I leafed through United's in-flight magazine, *Mainliner.* Finally I decided it was time for another iced tea.

"Maybe you're lonely here in the galley all by yourself," I suggested, as I joined her again, "and you might like some company."

"And you," she came back with a twinkle in her large, round eyes, "are the only single man on board. Right?"

"Right."

It was now or never. "What's your name?" I asked.

"Connie Butcher."

"I'm Brooks Robinson, but unless you follow baseball real close you wouldn't know me," I volunteered.

Throughout the rest of that six-hour trip I might as well have donned a stewardess's apron because I was in and out of that galley dozens of times.

We were almost over Boston before I mustered enough courage to find out what Connie's plans were once we arrived there.

"Could we have dinner tonight?" I asked. "We don't play tomorrow so there would be plenty of time."

"I'm not sure," she replied. "The crew may have to turn around tonight. We won't know until we check in at the terminal."

Shot down rather abruptly on that tack, I tried another. "Where are you staying tonight?" I wanted to know.

"At the Sheraton. Why don't you call me about an hour or so after we land? I'll know my schedule then."

I could hardly wait for that hour to pass. In fact, I tried the Sheraton in about forty-five minutes, but my eagerness went unrewarded. "Miss Butcher hasn't checked in," the operator told me.

At least I had the right hotel. There were two Sheratons in Boston but I hadn't had the foresight to find out which one Connie was staying in.

"We're staying over tonight," Connie gave me the news when we finally made connections fifteen long minutes later. I was on Cloud Nine when Connie agreed to have dinner with me. We ate at the Red Coach Inn, not far from the hotel, and when I dropped her off in the lobby later, I had the phone number of her apartment in Chicago, the city where she was based.

Jerry Walker was watching TV when I came in. I was so anxious to talk I fairly shouted down the actors in the late movie.

"Jerry," I proclaimed, "I've just met the girl I'm going to marry."

Jerry knew my date was with the stewardess on our flight from Kansas City, but that declaration left him temporarily speechless.

[127]

"Great, Brooks," he finally replied, as if to humor me. "But remember, you've got a few more games left this year before you can walk down the aisle."

I couldn't see that as the immediate problem. Besides, I was a thousand miles away thinking about what might have happened if Richards hadn't called me back from Vancouver. I wouldn't have been on the flight from Kansas City to Boston, and I wouldn't have met Connie.

Those few hours over dinner had been the most pleasant in my young life. We'd learned a lot about each other. Connie's full name was Constance Louise Butcher, and she was one of nine children. She'd been born in Detroit, where her family owned and operated a packaging firm known as Butcher Engineering. Five feet seven inches tall, and a slim hundred and twenty pounds, Connie had been homecoming queen in 1954 at the University of Detroit.

It was a pleasant surprise to find that she was something of a sports fan, too, even though she admitted she knew more about ice hockey than baseball since her dad and his brother owned the Windsor hockey club and also the Windsor Arena, in Canada, just across the bridge from Detroit.

The next day against the Red Sox, I had one of my best days of the year, going four for four. Bob Brown, our public relations director, still ribs me about that night and the apparent helpful effects on my play of love at first sight. Bob, as assistant traveling secretary to John Lancaster at the time, claims to have the date when Connie and I met— August 28, 1959—etched on his memory. He even tosses in the flight number of our plane when he talks about it, changing the number from time to time as the years go by.

When Connie left Boston for the return trip west, I was positive that she was the girl for me. The real question was whether she thought I was the right man for her. I could

[128]

hardly wait for the season to close, even though I continued to hit real well during September and closed out 1959 with a respectable .284 average.

As soon as I could get things packed after our last game, I piled into my new Chevrolet Impala and headed for Chicago. Many phone calls and letters had resulted in my planning my arrival to be there the day before Connie came in from a trip. Bob Hale, who'd been with me our first year at York and who played first base with the Orioles in place of Walt Dropo at times in 1959, lived near Midway Airport, and he'd asked me to stay with him. Connie was then living on the north side of Chicago not too far from Wrigley Field with two other stewardesses, Sonja Stumo and Judy Muncaster.

Connie didn't have a flight that week, and we had a wonderful time really getting to know each other. When the week was over and she had to go back to flying, I headed home for Little Rock with the promise that she would fly down to spend Christmas with us.

Although it seemed like a year from late September until the holidays, with all that long-distance courting and my required time in the National Guard, that winter flew by more quickly than any I can remember. The middle of February was there almost before I knew it.

I made plans to drive from Little Rock to Florida and spring training by way of Chicago. Even though Bob Hale had been sold to Cleveland during the winter, he again invited me to make his home my headquarters while I was there for a week's visit with Connie. Then just before I had to head south, Connie agreed to fly down to Florida with her sister for a few days.

Our engagement was a reality now. By midsummer, Connie quit United and went home to Windsor to get things arranged for our wedding. Setting a firm date was next to impossible, however, for the Orioles under Richards had really "arrived."

So many things happened to me between the close of the 1959 season in late September and October of 1960 it still doesn't seem possible. The feeling in my own mind was strong that I had actually arrived as a major league third baseman after coming back from Vancouver in July the year before. Then the final month of the season—after I met Connie—everything seemed to go right.

Spring training in 1960 was special. We still had seasoned players around like Gene Woodling, Hoyt Wilhelm, Gus Triandos, Walt Dropo, Clint Courtney, and Jim Busby. But mixed among them were a group that writers tagged as the "Baby Birds."

Jim Gentile, who was just twenty-six and had been acquired from the Dodgers, was slated for first base. Marv Breeding, back on second, wouldn't be twenty-six until March. Ronnie Hansen seemed a sure starter at shortstop and he would be only twenty-two in April. In terms of experience, I was the senior citizen of the Birds, and my twenty-third birthday wouldn't be until May 18.

At our very first meeting at camp, Paul Richards went out of character to talk at length about the White Sox rally to win the 1959 pennant away from the perennial champion New York Yankees in the closing days of the season. His confidence in our potential was evident. "We have the ability to do the same thing," he asserted, firmly.

Almost immediately, Richards decided to go with youth. Our starting rotation was made up of Milt Pappas, Jack Fisher, Chuck Estrada, Jerry Walker, and Steve Barber. All were twenty-two or a few weeks under when we arrived in

[130]

Florida. And the veterans among us, though up in years, all had what Richards demanded—desire to win.

Despite a slow start for me that year, by the time of our first road trip to Chicago things had improved on the field even though I was spending virtually every waking hour with Connie. I remember the White Sox manager, Al Lopez, telling the writers after I had taken away a sure hit from one of his players, "Brooks Robinson goes to his left better than anybody I've ever seen."

And it was in Chicago that my bat began to find its groove. I've always been an aggressive batter, swinging at a lot of pitches and sticking my head in tight over the plate. I hate to get behind a pitcher. I'd rather have him throwing good strikes to get me out rather than bad strikes for me to go fishing on.

Steadily improving my batting average, I had it up where it was an acceptable match with my glove by the end of June, and for the first time in my career I was selected as an All-Star third baseman. Once more there were two All-Star games within a three-day period—the first in Kansas City on July 11 and the next in New York two days later. It was one of the great personal thrills of my life to hear them announce, "Brooks Robinson, now playing third for the American League," even if I was filling in for starter Frank Malzone.

Four of the "Baby Birds" played that day, counting me, Ronnie Hansen, Chuck Estrada, and Jim Gentile. Even though we lost, 5–3, and I didn't get a hit in two at-bats, that dream that began in Little Rock and became reality in Kansas City Municipal Stadium still stands out as a great moment in my life.

Chicago continued to be my city that year. On our next

swing west, for some reason Connie couldn't get to the first game, probably because she was coming in from a trip. Just the same, I went five for five in that game with a home run, a triple, a double, and two singles—the first time I ever hit for the cycle.

At dinner with Connie later, we seemed to have so many important things to talk about that the subject of the game never came up. The next morning about eight o'clock or so Jerry Walker was shaking me conscious to answer the phone. It was Connie.

"Brooks Robinson," she screamed, abruptly startling me wide awake. "Why didn't you tell me last night that you made five hits? That was awful of you. I had to read it in the *Tribune* this morning."

Once I got oriented and found out it was so early, I tried to calm her down by telling her that baseball players who go five for five need their rest, but all it got me was a bang in the ear. She'd hung up.

The upset was only temporary, though, because it was later that day we decided to get married in October. Since we were still in the pennant race with the Yankees, however, we were going to have to wait a while to name the precise day. Even our wedding would have to be put aside if the Orioles made the World Series.

We went into the first days of September only two and a half games out of first, behind Casey Stengel's powerhouse. The names on that Yankee club are legendary: Tony Kubek, Gil McDougald, Roger Maris, Mickey Mantle, Yogi Berra, Clete Boyer, Bill Skowron, Bobby Richardson, Whitey Ford, Bob Turley, Bobby Shantz.

We had a three-game series on Labor Day weekend against Stengel's crew, and we won all three of them. The second win, 2–0, came on one of the big home runs of my life. I hit it in the eighth inning off Luis Arroyo, a fine left-handed relief pitcher who threw one of the great "scroogies," a reverse curve that was always tough for a right-handed batter, but especially so for me. But this one I got on the nose and drove deep into the seats in left field.

When New York left Baltimore after that series in second place by a half game, the town was talking about nothing but the "Baby Birds." No matter where we went we were mobbed. It was unbelievable. Here we were, a bunch of kids, really, and up in first place ahead of the Yanks. It was just like the dream I'd had on Denison Street in Little Rock when my only connection with the major leagues was the table model Philco radio and the box scores in the *Gazette*.

Less than two weeks later, we rode the train to New York for a four-game showdown series with the Yankees. New York, hanging right on our tail since we had swept that three-game set with them, had us all tied up in the American League, and the whole baseball world seemed to be after us.

The phone never quit ringing. We were interviewed by every radio and TV station in town, and the lobby was full of baseball writers not only from Baltimore and New York but other cities. It was pretty well concluded that whoever came out on top in this series would be in the World Series for the American League.

It was not to be our year. We lost all four. But we were in every game, even the finale of a Sunday doubleheader when we were shut out, 2–0. Though the season wasn't over, of course, we were a dejected bunch when we left New York. It would take a miracle for us to catch the Yanks, and when after that series they reeled off a long streak of fourteen in a row, that clinched it for them.

We ended up in second place, eight games out, but still a

tremendous jump ahead of sixth, where we'd been not too many weeks before. Even the fact that we'd all had a good year didn't make us feel any better. It's never a good year when you come so close, only to lose.

My average was .294 with fourteen home runs, 88 runs batted in, and a .977 average in the field.

The most impressive thing that happened to me in baseball, however, was running third in the voting that year for the most valuable player in the American League behind Roger Maris and Mickey Mantle. That was pretty classy company. And when Connie and I fixed our wedding date for October 8, it was with the realization that Brooks Robinson was finally established in the major leagues.

Chapter 17

Our wedding called for more planning and preparation than anything I've ever been through. The season's final out was hardly in the glove before I began a racehorse tour that found me writing innumerable notes to myself to make sure I wouldn't forget something. I had so many things to do there wasn't any other way. But the most important was to find a house or apartment to live in once we got back to Baltimore from our honeymoon.

Between the end of the season on the first Sunday in October and our wedding the following Saturday, we had the long-distance phone line between Baltimore and Detroit pretty well tied up over that problem. Finally, with Connie no better informed than my poor description over the phone would allow, I had to act on my own, and I purchased a house from L. G. Dupre, a former Baylor player then a halfback with the Baltimore Colts. I was confident that it had at least one good feature Connie couldn't argue with—its convenient location only ten blocks from Memorial Stadium.

The wedding was to take place at Christ the King Church in Windsor, Ontario. Connie's parents had a cottage there which fronted on Lake St. Clair, a beautiful fresh-water lake. Traffic was so heavy on the 500-mile journey from Baltimore via the Pennsylvania and Ohio Turnpike it's a wonder that I arrived safely and in condition to cope with the preparations that still remained. At least I got there in time for us to obtain the license and a permit from the archdiocese office that I as a Protestant had to sign in order to marry a Catholic. And, of course, we had to rehearse the wedding ceremony.

We were married by Monsignor Phillip Mugan on Saturday morning at 11 A.M. in a small traditional ceremony. Connie wore a beautiful long white wedding gown which her sister Pat had worn two months previously, and I had on a cutaway. Connie's sister Barbara was the bridesmaid and her husband served as best man. We were happy that my folks could make the long trip from Little Rock for the wedding and the immediate family reception that followed at the Elmwood Club.

Following the reception, we started our honeymoon trip by driving to Lake Tahoe. Even there, we couldn't quite escape the demands of a baseball career. When Norm Gerdman, a friend I had met while the Orioles were training in Scottsdale, asked me to speak at a banquet honoring the Little League program at Harrah's Club in Tahoe, I really couldn't refuse, and I was glad I hadn't.

Twenty or thirty other professional baseball players were

present, mainly from the San Francisco Giants and the Los Angeles Dodgers, plus hundreds of Little Leaguers. One of the greatest banquets for kids I've ever been around, it was held only that one year. The Commissioner of Baseball didn't feel the gambling permitted in the area was in keeping with the standards we were trying to set in general for the sport of baseball and, in particular, for the youngsters attending.

After a few days in Tahoe, we began to work our way back to the home in Baltimore that Connie had never seen. Our route took us through Yosemite, to Las Vegas, across the Southwest by way of Albuquerque, and ultimately to Little Rock, where we spent several days with my folks. Though Connie had visited briefly in Little Rock the previous Christmas, this was the first opportunity I'd had to show her Lamar Porter Field, downtown Little Rock, Travelers Stadium, the lake country, Hot Springs—all the places I'd talked about since we had met on that flight to Boston.

The next major stop on our itinerary was Detroit, where we had to pick up all of Connie's things. We looked more like a covered wagon than anything else when we left there with a U-Haul trailer in tow to drive the final lap to Baltimore. That trailer was nearly my undoing during the trip. To begin with, it took me several stops and starts to learn how to turn the car to make the trailer go where I wanted it. Then with the added hazard of almost continual rain, I nearly went off the highway a couple of times during the trip.

Perhaps we should not have timed our arrival for Halloween. As if to remind us of the approaching witching hour, that rain we'd brought along all the way whipped down even harder as we entered the city limits, obscuring Connie's first view of the row houses in our neighborhood. We made a mad dash from the car up the steps to 1503 Medford Road.

"Welcome home, Mrs. Robinson," I gasped when we got to the door.

Amazingly enough, I remembered to carry Connie over the threshold, though my difficulty getting the door open almost ruined the effort. It was fortunate I'd gotten the utilities turned on before I'd left Baltimore for the wedding. At least we had light and heat to counteract the effects of the ghostly appearance inside that near-empty house and the relentless downpour that drenched us on every one of our many trips to and from the car.

We still laugh about that night. We had to dig through boxes to find towels and bed linens before we could go to sleep. As a matter of fact, we were lucky to have a bed. That and a refrigerator were all I'd had time to buy before the wedding. But when you're young, it's lots easier to see the humor even in trying situations like that. Now if there are times when I can't find a bar of soap, I think the world is coming to an end.

The Dupres had left the drapes, and there were carpets on the floor. Except for our two pieces of furniture there wasn't another thing. Nothing to cook with. Nothing to eat with. In fact, there weren't even any hangers for our clothes.

What a lot of work was ahead of us to make a real home was all too evident in the cold light of day the next morning. And Connie's first real view of the row houses in that same daylight didn't do much to raise her spirits. She hadn't been acquainted with this type of architecture before. All houses share adjacent outside walls with their neighbors, so there are no side yards, and each house is one room and a hallway wide—about twenty-five feet overall. In our block of Medford Road, the row was three stories high; living room, dining room, and kitchen were on the entry level, with bedrooms above and basement below.

Those were the months of the lists. We had a list for everything, and slowly but surely we eliminated things that a house can't do without. Have you ever tried to hang a picture with no nails and no hammer? The heel of a shoe works pretty well for pounding, but there's no substitute for a nail.

After several weeks, things were in pretty good order. It was good not to have to sit on the floor to watch TV or to eat dinner standing up at the kitchen sink. But we were still missing something important, to our way of thinking.

Since Connie is from a large family and we both love kids, we wanted to get started on our family immediately. The project of getting one of the bedrooms ready for a nursery became a reality when Connie gave me the happy news that she was expecting our first child. Almost immediately she arranged a shopping expedition downtown with Peggy Wilhelm, wife of pitcher Hoyt Wilhelm, to select the crib and dresser and other essentials for the nursery.

By the time we had to leave for spring training at Miami, the nursery was ready. The doctor estimated Connie would deliver in July, any time from the 15th on. I wondered where I'd be when the moment arrived, and how I'd get the news from Detroit. Connie had gone there to be with her parents so she'd have someone to get her to the hospital.

Brooks David came into the world almost on schedule— about 11 A.M. on July 24, 1961, at Providence Hospital in Detroit. I will never forget that day. I was in Cooperstown playing in the Hall of Fame game and on third base when the public address announcer broke in during play to tell me and everyone else in the park that I was a father.

I didn't get to see Brooks David for nearly a week because of our game schedule. It wasn't until the All-Star game in Boston that I had a long enough break to make the trip to Detroit. After finishing my stint at third base, I left the game in the sixth inning and raced to the plane, barely making the only flight to Detroit that would give me time enough to see Connie and Brooks David that night.

Even before our second son, Chris, was born on February 22, 1963, we knew we had to find another house. Not only had we outgrown the row house, we lived too close to a heavily traveled street.

Ultimately we purchased a lot in Lutherville, a suburb about twelve miles north of Baltimore towards York, Pennsylvania. Connie and I spent weeks drawing floor plans, designing just the right house to fit our needs and the natural setting in our wooded area with low rolling hills. Our location, on a cul-de-sac, is ideal. It is quiet and affords the children a great place to romp and play.

When we finally moved from Medford Road in July 1964, it seemed to us as if we'd taken up residence in a resort hotel. Even though by this time we had a third addition to the family—Michael, born on March 11, 1964—our new home seemed unbelievably spacious. Making the adjustment from a tall, narrow row house to a 100-foot-wide four-bedroom rancher of perhaps 3000 square feet, sprawled across a large green lawn, was one of the more pleasant chores we've ever had.

The little Medford Road row house still brings back fond memories, nevertheless. We sold it to Dave McNally, one of Baltimore's great pitchers of the '70s. When he moved to Lutherville, he sold it to Curt Blefary, who used to play the outfield for us.

Diana was born on February 22, 1968. As the youngest in the family and our only girl, she was destined to be the fair-haired child. And, as might be expected, she has learned to keep all of us quite well lined up—even Mom and Dad.

Connie's task of keeping all four children on schedule is an arduous one. Nowadays with all three boys involved in Little League, school, church, and other activities, she's almost a full-time chauffeur. It seems she's always driving someone somewhere. I try to relieve her of some of that responsibility when I'm home during the season, and in the off-season, of course, a good deal of that driving falls to me. It's lucky I enjoy driving, and I really appreciate being with the children since I'm gone so much from April through September.

Though we've taken all of them to spring training for years, that day is rapidly coming to an end. We don't feel we should take them out of school after grammar school age, and that day has already arrived for Brooks David. But to compensate for my being gone so much, we try to do a lot of things as a family when we have the opportunity. I don't want the kids to grow up wondering if I'm for real.

Each one of the children is a distinct individual, a normal situation in most families, I'm sure. And in common with other parents, Connie and I get a day-to-day—really, hour-to-hour—practical lesson in child psychology as we try to learn how to handle each of them. Connie is a wonderful mother; she never seems to get mad. I'm a pretty patient guy, too, they tell me, but I do set the law down from time to time.

All three boys have an interest in sports. Right now, Brooks David, being the oldest, is the most knowledgeable. Only time will tell which one has the most ability, however. Michael is what I call a typical third son. He never wants to be left out of anything Brooks David and Chris are doing, and he is the most mischievous of the three.

Chris may be the mechanic in the family. He loves to work with his hands. He's always building something and seems to understand what makes things work. I hope that aptitude continues to develop to the point where he can fix the light switches and doorknobs that his dad can't. He's quiet and even-tempered most of the time, but when he gets mad—well, the others had better just clear a path.

Diana, who is able to get her way most of the time, is obviously the queen. Michael and Diana, who are the closest in age, seem to be at each other all the time.

We enjoy the kids. Now that they are all older and easier to handle, we go a lot of places together. As all parents know, when one or two are very young, it's a chore just to move around. The historic sites in the Washington and Baltimore area are frequent targets of our interest. We have a lot up in Gettysburg where we often go. Some day we hope to build a summer home there, but at present we have to be satisfied with spending some of my off-days in the summer there swimming and hiking.

Kids are amazing. They learn so fast that it's hard to keep ahead of them. And you certainly can't anticipate what they're going to say next.

I'll never forget the day several years ago when Brooks David came home from Mount Washington Country School and really jumped me about something he'd learned there.

"Hey, dad," he confronted me. "Some of the kids in my class say you're really something special playing third base for Baltimore. Why didn't you tell me that you were famous?"

One Sunday several years ago, as we were getting ready to leave for church, Brooks David turned to his mother and asked, "Why doesn't Daddy go to church with us?" And before either of us could answer, he went on, "Why does he always go to his own church?"

I'd gone to church all my life. Our family attended Capitol View Methodist Church in Little Rock, and after Connie and I were married, I went regularly to Waverly Methodist Church in Baltimore. Gradually we had settled into a pattern where Connie would go to Mass with the children and I would go alone to my own services.

I'd thought about this occasionally through the years and once or twice had even talked to other people with religiously mixed marriages. Some of the people I talked to had eventually become Catholics, and most agreed it had worked out fine. So, after trying to explain to Brooks David why I went to one church and he and his brothers and sister and mother went to another, I decided it was time to evaluate things. Perhaps it would be better if we were all to go to the same service as a family.

But I felt the need for counsel. For, while my Christian faith is very important to me, I don't consider myself a student of theology. Actually, my faith far overshadows my intellectual understanding of Christianity. I believe in Jesus Christ, and Christianity, thanks to my parents, has been a part of my life as long as I can remember.

Father Martin Schwalenberg, a close friend but not our parish priest, seemed the right person to turn to. I couldn't have chosen anyone more fair to help me analyze my situation. Putting no pressure on me whatsoever to become a Catholic, he simply pointed out how good it would be for our family to worship together. I became convinced that I could feel at home in the Catholic church. For me there is one absolute—Jesus Christ. The rest of us are still trying to reach his spiritual perfection, and that's the significant goal, no matter what form our worship takes.

Father Schwalenberg continued to be helpful. As a matter of convenience, since his house was so near ours, he provided the instruction required of me before I would formally be converted to Catholicism.

Through the years our schedule for professional baseball had always been a hindrance when it came to regular church attendance. Although the hour of service had never been a problem for me as I was growing up, even as a minor league player I experienced difficulties getting to church. At most Methodist churches, the usual hour for services was around 11 A.M., but by that time I almost always had to be at the ball park. Now, however, I can always find an early Mass wherever I am, so I seldom miss a service.

Anyone who knows me more than casually is aware that I consider religion and politics matters for individual discretion. I never try to force my views onto someone else, but I'm always glad to respond to a question about my personal beliefs. There is one place, however, where I'm always more than willing to speak—for the Fellowship of Christian Athletes, of which I've been a member for almost as long as I've been in organized baseball. George Kell, the first person I ever heard speak at one of their meetings, made a tremendous impression on me when he addressed a capacity audience at Emmanuel Baptist Church in Little Rock in 1957 or 1958. As he talked about baseball, his career, and the importance of Christianity in his life, I realized for the first time what an influence professional athletes can have, particularly on young people. I have been an enthusiastic supporter of FCA ever since.

Speaking at FCA meetings—something I do four or five times a year—seems more important today than ever before. Even though young people have been exposed to a far greater bulk of factual knowledge and are a lot more sophisticated about life than I was when I first got into professional baseball, temptations are no easier to resist. Young athletes are especially vulnerable to their circumstances. The long periods of time that they are away from home, the excessive adulation of admiring fans, and the heightened emotional stress of game conditions are all hazards to any kind of normal life.

If there is any advice that I could give here to young ball players—whether they have pro ambitions or whether they just play the game for pure pleasure—I think I would emphasize two words: *time* and *believe*.

Take *time* to search within yourself, to know yourself more fully so that you may relate to those around you in a better way. Take the time to listen and to understand the problems that we all have. Take the time to thank everyone who has helped you in any way down the avenue of success in your particular endeavor.

The word *believe* means many things. Try to understand how much ability you really have. Learn to appreciate what God has given you. Develop the ability to believe in yourself. Associate with those who help you believe and who provide you with the confidence you need to achieve your goals.

To believe means also to understand other people's problems. Remember, your problems aren't the only ones. Be an optimist; in fact, make optimism a way of life for you.

Trial and tribulation will be with us along much of the way we must walk through life, and it will be impossible to take a single step forward without strong, deep-seated faith. My commitment to Jesus Christ who tells me that I can withstand all things through him gives me the courage I need to face whatever life may bring. And if I fail to meet its challenges in the way he wants me to, I know he is ready with forgiveness and the promise that I may still become a new person through him.

I've tried in these few pages to express my basic views on life and religion. They may not necessarily fit anyone else, but they fit me and they have enabled me to live within the rigors of my profession. I hope some of the things I've said both here and at FCA conferences about the importance of Christ in my life have been of help to others. I know that sharing my faith has helped me grow as a person.

Chapter 19

Baseball has been my life. I've loved it and played it almost as long as I can remember. And it's given me more good memories to treasure than I can possibly recall. I wouldn't want to change that.

But life isn't one-sided, and we have our share of problems in baseball. I've had a pretty close look at them, too, as a player representative off and on since 1960. And in any discussion of an issue about which I feel strongly, whether it's on my own or in behalf of our own club's players or as spokesman for all the American League clubs to the Players' Association, I'm probably one of the most vocal participants.

One of my biggest personal gripes is the travel schedule, although that's better now than it used to be. We still have a long way to go, however, and it seems unlikely that much further progress can be made until management cuts down on the number of games we play each season. From the 154 per year that we had when I first came to the big leagues, the figure in our circuit has gone to 162 as a result of the expansion to fourteen clubs in 1961. That overloaded schedule has been the chronic gripe of the players over the years, and the basic cause for the often unrealistic demands of our travel schedule.

I once knew a conductor on the railroad who was always looking at his watch and timetable to see where he'd be next. Today's baseball player has to do the same thing with his travel itinerary. Sometimes I even wake up with a start and wonder if I have overlooked some essential part of that mimeographed schedule we follow so closely. It's so full it would be easy to become confused.

The club traveling secretary Phil Itzoe handles the actual details of our trip planning just fantastically. Everything that relates to travel—hotel accommodations and so on—is set down in black and white in the agreement between the Players' Association and the owners. The itinerary given to each of us making a road trip contains complete information on all arrangements—even down to such questions as whether we pack our bag and leave it in the lobby of the hotel at 9 A.M. or whether it goes with us on the bus to the park.

Packing that bag, incidentally, is much easier than it used to be in the days of train travel. I've got it down almost to a science where everything goes into one three-suiter. Almost all my suits, sport coats and slacks are double knits, so they don't have to be pressed. Shirts and shorts are wash and wear, and most of my shoes are patent leather and can be cleaned with a damp cloth. Actually, we don't have any excuses left for not meeting Earl Weaver's grooming standards.

When we are leaving from Baltimore, we give our personal luggage to the clubhouse man who sees that it gets on a truck to go with the baseball gear out to our plane. Once we arrive at our destination, another truck picks everything up from the plane. The equipment is dropped off at the park and our personal luggage goes to the hotel where the bellman delivers each player's bags to his preassigned room.

Undoubtedly the current energy crisis will have its effect on baseball, perhaps even accomplishing the changes in schedule and travel that we've been arguing about so long. Playing ten games in ten days in three cities with no day off as we do on occasions may very well become a thing of the past. We went extra innings in the final game of one such trip I remember and had to rush like mad to make a plane that took off at 12:15 A.M. for Baltimore. We landed around 4:30 in the morning. By the time we got our luggage and headed home the sun was up. Since the kids wanted to see me, I stayed up until they'd gotten up and we'd had a chance to be together for a little while. It was nearly eight o'clock when I went to bed. When Connie woke me about three, I hadn't even begun to catch up on my sleep. But if I was to have anything to eat and still make it to the park by four, I had to get up anyway.

I can remember times even worse than that, when we've had to be back at the park in midafternoon for a twi-night doubleheader after having been as late as ten in the morning getting home from a trip. No wonder we sometimes play like zombies.

One of the greatest difficulties that ever arose between players and management, of course, was the Curt Flood case and the huge hassle over the reserve clause. That came in 1969 when I was the Oriole player representative for the Players' Association. While I've never really been concerned about being a free agent myself because I've been so happy in Baltimore, I supported Curt Flood both from an individual standpoint as well as the players' standpoint. As most of them do, I feel strongly that the reserve clause should be changed. It binds a player to a club for life or until that club decides to trade him or release him.

I hate to hear a player say, "I'm a hundred-thousand-dollar slave," or, "I'm a prisoner." That doesn't set well with me. But in a sense that's exactly what he is now. Back when I signed with Baltimore in 1955, the choice of club was mine. Today a prospect doesn't have that option. He is drafted and must either sign with that club or not play ball at all.

Now, I'm for every owner getting every cent out of baseball that he has put into it, and with a reasonable profit, if possible. I realize full well that it costs a club over a million dollars a year to develop young talent. Baseball, with the farm system it sustains to teach young prospects how to play this game, is different from any other pro sport in that respect.

But somewhere along the line I feel there should be a modification in the reserve rules. Sometime, somewhere in his career, a player should have a say as to what his future holds for him. It is a tough problem with no easy solution acceptable to both sides.

Again in 1972 I was American League player representative when another major disagreement came to a head. We struck for ten days then in an effort to solve our pension problems, and it was the worst ten days of my life. The players had to take the brunt of the public reaction. We simply didn't, and don't, have the money, the organization, or the facilities to present our case as well as the owners do theirs.

Fans looked upon us as ogres of some kind for going on

strike. When they've worked hard all week and want to see a game, they don't want to find the ball park closed up. They put sports on a plane so far removed from reality they forget that the players are human too. And, when the spokesman for the players happens to make $100,000 a year—which was true in my case—they resent hearing him talk about baseball's problems, even though his complaints are made on behalf of twenty-four other players too. They forget that superstar salaries are the exception rather than the rule.

During the player strike, one of the letters in the Baltimore paper pointed out that I owned a restaurant and a sporting goods store. "I wonder," asked the writer of the letter, "if Brooks Robinson gives his employees as good a pension plan and fringe benefits as he demands for himself from his employer."

Another wrote: "The way I feel about Robinson now, I might boycott his sporting goods store and his restaurant."

Certainly I would have preferred to have been elsewhere than arguing as player representative with management just then. But when you think you are right, you do what you think is right, and I was speaking for a lot of players, not just for myself.

Baseball is a wonderful game and a wonderful way of life. But the players have had a lot of catching up to do and the problems are not all obvious. We're in pretty good shape now, and I'm reasonably sure there will never again be another strike like that one. Owners simply haven't been used to listening to the other side of the story, but they've begun to realize baseball is as much the players' game as it is theirs. Now that we know each other a lot better I think we'll be able to sit down together and resolve most of our difficulties.

Our problems are really just like those faced by farmers,

or doctors, or truck drivers, or corporation executives—that list could go on and on. The only difference is that we live in front of a giant mirror into which the whole world can look every day. All of us in baseball are concerned about the image of the game that we project there. Naturally we expect some adverse reaction; that is inevitable for anything on public display. But we hope enough public understanding exists now to enable us to improve our "fringe package," as it is usually called, without becoming whipping boys for the less tolerant of our critics.

I love baseball. It's an intriguing game—as simple and yet as complicated as when Abner Doubleday created it years ago before any of us playing it now were born—and it's survived many problems quite successfully. We're glad that's true, because all of us who are in it love being here. We hope future generations can look back on our years and see something of benefit in what we've done. Most of all, we want to make sure the game is still here getting better and better for them to enjoy as we have.

Chapter 20

A great many people look at baseball players as being wealthy men. A lot of us do make a fine living, but the great majority struggle just to get along. People read that the minimum wage is $15,000, and that sounds great. But have you tried maintaining two homes, sometimes three, on that kind of salary? There has to be one wherever home may really be; another in the city where your team is based; and then an interim location for spring training.

There is no way a player earning baseball's minimum salary is going to save any money. He can make ends meet by careful managing, but that's all. Only after he has established himself and his salary begins improving steadily can he begin to save and accumulate a nest egg. But since most of us baseball players have so little business sense or experience, we find it difficult to manage our resources to the best advantage. I realized that long ago and tried to get guidance from my father-in-law, my lawyer, and other people whose understanding I respected.

Players with popular appeal and, presumably, proven ability, are presented with business opportunities from time to time. They can sign up for all kinds of endorsements from bubble gum cards to TV commercials. They can get involved in the restaurant business and sporting goods, as I did, or in any number of other investments. The question is to find which ones are best in each individual situation.

I've been involved in a lot of things in the way of endorsements and business ventures since I first signed with Rawlings Sporting Goods and Topps Bubble Gum way back in my first year in baseball. The Rawlings contract has worked out well for me and Topps Bubble Gum has been good to all the players. In return for allowing our pictures to be used on the trading cards the kids swap back and forth, we get $250 a year or the right to select merchandise of that value from a gift brochure. I can remember vividly the zeal with which I collected those cards when I played baseball in Little Rock as a boy, not to mention the amount of bubble gum I chewed. Maybe that has something to do with the number of baseball players seen blowing bubbles during televised games.

My first major involvement was as partner in a restaurant located quite close to Baltimore's Memorial Stadium. At first it was Brooks and Eddie Robinson's Gorsuch House, but now it is identified by my name only, since Eddie, who used to play first base for the Orioles, has been out of the business for some time.

I'm still partners with George Henderson in a sporting goods store now located in Lutherville close to my home. A third partnership enterprise—a summer sports camp for kids—proved to be too much for Wesley Unsell and me to handle. It was a great experience, but coming as it did during baseball season, both Wesley (who played with the Baltimore Bullets) and I had to get out after a year.

As the practice of employing business managers to handle all types of professional athletes became increasingly popular, I decided to investigate the pros and cons of that solution to my own problems. The more complicated things became at the restaurant, the more obvious it was that I needed help—professional help—to keep me out of trouble. And as I was bombarded with more and more endorsement requests, I finally concluded that I was a fish out of water in the business world and that I'd better do something about it. I needed more than an accountant and an attorney; I needed a business manager.

So in 1969—fourteen years into baseball—I became the first major league player to sign with International Merchandising Corporation. That's a highfalutin title, but what it really amounted to was that Brooks Robinson was obtaining the business skills of Mark McCormack, the business management consultant whose group first gained public notice for its handling of golfer Arnold Palmer.

Every aspect of my business—including my contracts with the Orioles, all endorsement agreements, any paid personal appearances, even the contract to write this book —is handled by Mark's firm. In fact, they take care of everything having to do with money for me and my family. All my income, from whatever source, is paid directly to International Merchandising Corporation. We—Connie and I and all the kids—are then given a monthly allowance to live on. All our bills—for light and for water, the charge ticket from the gas station, Connie's shopping tour at the department store, the dentist's statement—go to McCor-

mack. Once a month we get an itemized account of all trans-
actions—bills paid and the amount, monies received, such
as my check from the Orioles, and other monies paid out.

My introduction to Mark goes all the way back to 1957,
indirectly, and the winter ball I played that year in Cuba.
Eddie Thompson was then the golf pro at the Havana
Country Club, where I played a lot of golf, and I got to
know Eddie well when I lived right next door to him and
his family in Havana. Later, after Eddie had become the
pro at Sea Island, Georgia, the subject of athlete management firms came up in a conversation we were having. Eddie
said he was familiar with McCormack's group and knew
Mark McCormack personally. I'd heard of them, of course,
because of the work they had done with Arnold Palmer,
Jack Nicklaus, and Gary Player.

Although the firm at this time was handling only golfers,
they were thinking about branching out into other sports, so
Eddie wrote me a letter of introduction to Mark. Right
after we finished the World Series in 1969, I flew to Cleveland to talk over our situation with Connie's dad. Our con-
clusion was that McCormack's advice and counsel would
be of significant value to me and that I ought to engage
the services of the firm.

By this time, they'd signed Stan Mikita, a great star
with the Chicago Blackhawks in the National Hockey
League and several basketball players. Ultimately they
signed Jeannie Shrimpton, the famous model; Chris
Schenkel, the sportscaster; Peter Revson, the super race
driver; and many others.

I've never regretted my decision to engage McCormack's
firm. Everything I consider as an investment or for mone-
tary gain they evaluate. They provide me also with other
proposals, evaluations, and their recommendations. I go
along with most of their ideas.

Although my paid personal appearances are set up by McCormack, there are other appearances I handle myself. I feel strongly that public sports figures must not only support our own area of interest but provide a helping hand to the many others less fortunate than we. Most groups can't afford to give us anything but appreciation for our appearances. We really receive much more than we give when we share something of ourselves with organizations like Little League, churches, hospitals, and the many charitable groups that call on us from time to time.

I remember one such affair that moved me very deeply. It was an awards presentation held at a Baltimore bowling alley for the local chapter of Multiple Sclerosis, of which I am a director. My schedule was quite open that Saturday so I got there forty-five minutes or an hour ahead of time. About twenty MS victims who had taken part in a bowling league of their own—some of them in wheel chairs—were there already. The effort they had to expend just to participate in such an activity must have been tremendous. But with all their problems, those men and women were joking and needling each other about gutter balls, missed tenth pins and the like—things you would never expect from people in such handicapped physical condition.

It wasn't long before I was kidding some of them about their scores. They came back at me like tigers, most of them giving me a bad time about my hair. It recedes a bit, and no ball player ever got on me better than that group. It was a thrill to see them take advantage of their situation instead of letting their handicap keep them from having fun. Experiences like this really make me appreciate the physical ability and health God has given me.

Of all the personal appearance tours I've ever been on, one in 1967 made the greatest impact on me. Several baseball players, including Joe Torre and Hank Aaron of Atlanta and Harmon Killebrew of the Minnesota Twins, were in the group led by Stan Musial. Formerly with the Cardinals, he had retired from active play and become a vice president of that organization.

We toured Vietnam for seventeen days and went from one end of the country to the other, mostly in the field and at base hospitals, visiting the wounded. Since the trip took place in the first part of 1967, just a few months after we'd won our first World Series in four straight, we had a film of those games along, of course. That's the year we beat a great Dodger club headed by two of the toughest pitchers I've ever batted against—Sandy Koufax and Don Drysdale. We were in and out of helicopters, got a couple of bullet holes in a C-130, and dined with VIPs like Generals Walt and Westmoreland. But the greatest impression I came home with was of the patients in the hospitals.

In a base hospital near Da Nang that Musial and Aaron and I visited, they had just brought in a young soldier who had stepped on a land mine. You could tell that he was in terrible pain. One of his legs was gone and the other badly mangled. The doctors said they might have to amputate the remaining leg.

As the soldier—really just a boy—tried to raise a glass of water up to his mouth, he found he couldn't do it. One of the others—I think it was Aaron—did it for him.

An attending doctor asked if he knew who we were.

"No," he said.

"This is Brooks Robinson . . . Hank Aaron . . . Stan Musial," the doctor said, introducing each of us in turn.

The soldier started apologizing for not recognizing us. Imagine—here was this boy with one leg gone and the other perhaps about to be amputated, and he was concerned about our feelings at not being recognized. I don't know about the others, but I had to fight against tears.

While on that tour, whenever I ran into servicemen from Baltimore and Detroit, I took phone numbers of their parents, family, or friends. Returning first to Detroit where Connie and the kids had spent the time while I was gone, I made ten or fifteen phone calls to families there and in nearby Michigan. Then in Baltimore I completed a similar number, to let those people know I had seen their son or nephew or grandson, or whatever the case was.

I'd fired a gun or two in training in the Arkansas National Guard, but I'd never had anyone shooting back at me in anger. Seeing the results of war leaves you in a cold sweat, and we wondered what lay ahead for those poor victims confined to hospital beds. Maybe Musial, Torre, Aaron, Killebrew and I might have great skill as baseball players, but we were minor leaguers or less when it came to doing much for any of these patients.

Almost worse than the wounds and actual maiming we saw during our tour in the war zone was seeing the growing drug addiction among servicemen. In every hospital we saw wards where young soldiers—many of them teenagers —were trying to be rehabilitated. I've been concerned about drugs ever since the problem began its rise in the United States. When I first came into baseball, alcohol was the main vice. Drugs were nowhere around. Now all you hear about from high schoolers (and some younger students) is marijuana and even the hard drugs.

Words aren't potent enough opposition for hard drugs, but I try to make mine count for everything I can whenever I can. I do a lot of speaking to youth groups about the results of drug usage, especially as related to baseball. Dependent upon superior timing and reflex rather than power and strength, baseball is a tough sport under the best of circumstances, and drugs of any kind seriously hinder your play. With 162 games from April through September, baseball is a day-to-day job, and anyone who thinks he can keep hyping himself up to play better is dreaming.

Some years ago during spring training in Fort Lauderdale, a medical expert from Johns Hopkins Medical School in Baltimore spoke to all the player representatives about drugs, their problems, and their impact on baseball. It was an eye-opening experience for me and most of the other representatives.

I want no part of the drug scene, and I'm convinced that no one—especially an athlete—can afford to become involved in any way. Playing around with drugs will surely destroy whatever talents God has given us.

21

Playing professional baseball is not just a February to September affair. The importance of conditioning—both physical and mental—has become more and more apparent to me as the years passed. Quite early in my career, I discovered that if I was going to stick in the big leagues and achieve continued success, I had to prepare myself almost on a year-round basis.

That meant workouts. It is impossible to go out on the field and play major league ball without tremendous preparation, no matter what your age. But there is no doubt that this emphasis must increase with the years. Now I do my unwinding between the close of baseball season and the Christmas holiday. But once the tree in the living room has been taken down and the holiday spirit at the Robinson household is tucked away for another year, I go to work.

Nowadays I work almost as hard during the off season as in season, doing a great deal of my pre-season conditioning at the YMCA in Towson, a Baltimore suburb adjacent to Lutherville. Starting January 2, those of us who live in the area check into the Y on a daily basis to get in shape.

Billy Hunter, our third base coach, supervises our programs. He's a demanding taskmaster when it comes to getting ready for spring training.

In addition to an extensive exercise regime, we do a lot of running and play a lot of basketball at the Y. The past two or three years, the Orioles have had a basketball team that plays 10 to 15 games in the area, usually to help in some fund-raising effort for a high school or a civic club. Actually organized by the players, it is a pretty good team, with Jim Palmer, Paul Blair, and Merv Rettenmund among the "regulars." We didn't lose a game last year. (Of course, our success could result from the fact that the greater share of the time our competition is with faculty members and we should be in better physical condition than most of them.)

I've always stayed in good shape during the winter but now, more than ever, I really work at it. Even during my "holiday" between the end of the season and January 2, I do some jogging around the neighborhood one or two days a week, and I feel better when I do it. Not only does it keep my body toned but, most important, it keeps my legs in shape.

The legs and feet are all-important to an athlete. An athlete is only as good as he can move and no one moves anywhere without his legs and his feet. Although I've always believed that I would be able to tell when I was over the hill by my fielding more than my hitting, I think I've changed my view in the last year or two. I still feel I can get almost any ball that I could have reached ten years ago.

Now the test will come when I just can't hit that baseball any more.

Currently there is a lot of emphasis on weight training. I'm one baseball player who takes exception to the importance placed upon it. I don't believe in weight-lifting because I've always felt it would mess up my playing style. Mine is a loose type of play, but it does require some work with hand grips to keep my hands, wrists, and forearms strong.

One often ignored aspect of conditioning is diet. I try to stabilize my weight throughout the year by eating lightly and not too often. I do eat a lot of meat, but avoid desserts and sweets. I love salad and I've got to be a walking, talking commercial for iced tea since I drink it winter, summer, spring, and fall. Connie once remarked she wouldn't be at all surprised to see me drinking it in a snowstorm.

A little ritual I've perpetuated ever since 1960 is proof of my concern with maintaining a stable weight. When I check in on the first day of spring training I go to the scales and weigh myself. On a light beige tile wall in the trainer's quarters in Miami Stadium I write the record of my self-control: I've been anywhere from 190 to 193 or 194 each year.

Still, I'm hardly a walking collar ad. Even though God endowed me with a comparatively slim frame, I've never been able to keep a little roll off my waist. In Florida early for spring training one year, I went by to see Charlie Lau, a catcher off and on with the Orioles, who was already there working on a construction job. I was in my regular Florida uniform—a T shirt, some nice, baggy but comfortable walking shorts and tennies—as the kids call tennis shoes these days.

Charlie was always needling me about my shape. This

day was no different as we joshed around. Later on Charlie told me about the reaction of the men working with him.

"He's the All-Star third baseman?" one of them asked, unbelieving.

"Yeah," Charlie confirmed.

"In the big leagues?"

"That's right."

"Well," Charlie related his friend's estimate between big bursts of laughter, "then we've all got a chance to play for Baltimore. I'll tell you this, if you two are examples of what the Orioles have to play with, I'm picking the Yankees."

Some of the larger fellows find it hard to get by on the per diem allowance we receive when we are on the road ($19 per day in 1973). A major portion of that goes for food. Meals in some of our cities—New York is the prime example—can be horrendous. I can see where a big man, say, like Earl Williams or Boog Powell, who needs a lot of food to fire up that engine of his, can consistently overspend in New York without much effort.

I eat a good breakfast—bacon, eggs, toast and perhaps tea. Then about three or so, depending upon when the game starts, I eat my lunch-dinner, as I call it. That can be a big salad, or a hamburger with the trimmings, or, sometimes, a small dinner steak. No matter what it is, it's always topped off with two or three glasses of iced tea.

Normally, my third meal comes in the clubhouse, not because I want to save a dollar but mainly because it is pretty tough to find any place to eat after a night game. In Baltimore I usually eat at home after the game—sometimes a snack, sometimes a large meal. It's usually after 11 P.M. before we leave the clubhouse.

Over the years, the attendants for the visiting clubhouse

have become very professional in serving "spreads." Now every club in the American League—and I presume in the National League too—puts one out. It's a regular buffet with cold cuts, bread, pickles, olives, relishes, soft drinks, and iced tea.

The champion provider of all the visiting clubhouse attendants, Jimmy Wisner in Minnesota, may have been the one who started the whole thing five or six years ago. The secret to Jimmy's culinary success is his mother's cooking. Her fried chicken, hot casserole dishes, and salads really hit the spot.

In addition to setting out the spreads, Jimmy is one of the finest clubhouse men in seeing that everything is in place when you come to the game and anything you ask of him is done immediately. When thirty players are all asking for something it can be quite a feat to keep up with them.

Fortunately, each clubhouse manager has three or four aspiring youngsters around to help him. Almost all of them hope to play big league ball, and every once in a while one or two make it. Rene Lachemann, a catcher for the Athletics when they were in Kansas City, was a good example. He had worked in the visiting team clubhouse at Dodger Stadium when the Angels played there.

Youngsters like these are a joy to be around. They're so interested in baseball they will do anything in the world for you. Like Rene, a lot of them have a great deal of talent and I'm sure being around the clubhouse doesn't hurt them any.

The Orioles' organization emphasizes personal appearance both at home and on the road. Earl Weaver has a rule that we are always to be properly dressed in a public area. That means a coat, shirt, and tie at all times on the road. The only place we can take off our ties is in our rooms.

But if we set foot outside that door, we'd better be wearing a tie or run the chance of being fined.

As player representative, I have had numerous discussions with Earl about the shirt-and-tie rule. Some of the players would like to be able to wear turtlenecks or sport shirts, but Earl is adamant. In one of our discussions I thought I'd made some real points for turtlenecks and open-throated sport shirts. "If I permit that," Earl resisted, "next thing you know I'm going to be walking through the lobby some day and there'll be one of my guys in one of those night-gowns."

That almost broke me up. But it was only a day or so later that a man wearing one of them walked past me in a hotel lobby. Really caftans, they'll never be anything but "nightgowns" to Weaver nor permissible to wear anywhere but in your bedroom—if there.

Though I have no personal objections to the coat-and-tie rule, many players do. We even adhere to it in spring training in Florida after 6 P.M., and sometimes it's broiling hot down there. We have few hair restrictions, as long as it is neat. No beards are permitted, but mustaches are all right if they too are kept neat.

The only other club with regulations close to ours is Cincinnati, and, if anything, they are even more strict. Cincinnati is a coat-and-tie club, too, with strict hair-length regulations and no hair on the face permitted. That's Sparky Anderson's rule. If you want to play for the Reds you play it his way. With the success both Weaver and Anderson have had, it's pretty hard to knock their stand.

If there is anything at all about being a major league ball player that I don't enjoy, it's the problem of getting a little lonesome on the road. Reading helps, I find. I always take a book along, usually a historical novel or some other good reading to help me unwind before going to sleep or to occupy free time during the day.

Continuing friendships formed over the years in different cities have helped alleviate the lonesomeness to some extent, of course. In Minnesota, for instance, I see Gordon Sudin, a pitcher who broke in with me at York. He had a super fast ball but hurt his arm and that was it. Out in Oaklard, from time to time I see Dr. Charles Norlinger, a physician formerly from Little Rock, and my old roomie, Frank Zupo, a catcher in our organization. And I enjoy unexpectedly running into old friends in a city; it makes that stop just a little more interesting.

Even so, on the road there is a lot of time to fill. You can read only so long, watch so much TV, play only so much gin rummy with Billy Hunter, lobby-sit so long, do so much window-shopping, and eat only so much food. During the great chess match between Bobby Fischer and Boris Spassky, a lot of baseball players took up the game. I was among them, but my oldest son, Brooks David, can whip me easily.

As the years go by I find myself going out to the park earlier and earlier. Sometimes I just relax and get mentally ready to play the game. If I'm not hitting real well, which seems ultimately to be the problem of all ball players, I take some extra batting practice.

But almost every activity I participate in is directed toward one goal—staying in the best possible shape. That's the only way, in my opinion, you can make the major leagues in the first place and it's definitely the only way to remain here.

Playing the game of baseball is an individual matter. Sure, our uniforms are similar, and we all have spikes on our shoes, wear the same kind of caps and helmets, and use similar gloves. Everyone subscribes to the same general theory of baseball, and strategies differ very little. But the intimate part of the game rests with each person who plays it. Each of us has a style all his own. Who's to say which is right and which is wrong?

Now the Brooks Robinson style of playing third base is quite different from most. Though I've never played ice hockey, I feel that playing third is almost like being goalie on a hockey club. You aren't responsible for much ground but you need quick reflexes and you have to be willing to stick your chin out in front of the ball—if necessary, to let that ball bounce off your body if it can't be handled cleanly.

There's no easy lesson to playing a particular position in any sport. Even after more than three thousand games in my lifetime so far, I don't set myself up as a professor of third base. But one principle is positive. You must concentrate to play third, second, short, or any position, for that matter. Whenever I goof up a play or make an error there's one answer—lack of concentration.

Still indelible on my mind, although it happened several years back, is an incident that took place in Kansas City sometime before the Athletics' move to Oakland in 1968. Gino Cimoli was with the A's then, and in the first inning he dropped an easy bunt down the line. Getting to the ball late, I threw wildly, and Jim Gentile at first couldn't get to it. It was my first error in thirty-four games, I remember that.

Why did I do it?

I wasn't concentrating. I was thinking about my shoes.

I had on the wrong pair. Just as I use one glove to practice and another glove to play, I wear one pair of shoes for practice and one pair for play, and I had forgotten to put on my game shoes. Not until I got set for the first pitch did I notice anything wrong. But when I glanced down at my feet, I realized I hadn't changed my shoes.

Now when you're out there on the field you can't think of anything but baseball. I know I must always think ahead of every pitch. "If the ball is hit to me," I ask myself, "where's my play? What are my options if men are on base? Where's the preferred throw?"

And the reason I blew the throw on Cimoli was that I was wondering whom I could get to run back to the clubhouse and get my playing shoes, not what Gino might do up there at bat.

Concentration is vital.

[169]

The best defensive third baseman I've seen in my eighteen plus years in the majors is Clete Boyer. He spreads out, hunches down, and waits for the ball to be hit. But I play the bag differently from him or anyone else, I guess. I want movement in my body. When the pitcher throws, my body is in motion toward the plate. It's kind of like standing on a wall and seeing how far you can move forward without falling off.

That's the motion I want. I want to be moving forward but not committed to go straight ahead or left or right. That happens after the ball is hit. Eight out of ten times, I can tell when a man is going to bunt; then I really want forward motion. Most batters tip off their bunt attempts. They just don't look the same in the box. They do some little thing differently, and after a while you put those things down in your mental book.

Only a few give nothing away. Nellie Fox was one of the masters at bunting. In all the years I played against him, I never knew when he was going to bunt. Larry Brown on our club was that kind of bunter when he was with the Cleveland Indians.

Because of batters like Fox and Brown a third baseman has to be prepared for anything. He must also master a variety of throws. Generally, it's best to throw with a three-quarter arm motion. Not only does this allow accuracy, but it makes it possible to get more on the ball. At other times, for example on a double play to second base, a sidearm throw is required. And 99 percent of the time on a bunt the ball must be scooped up and fired underhand.

That technique is really important on what we call "swinging bunts," where the batter takes a full cut and taps the ball down the third-base line. On those, with the batter already running to first, the third baseman must grab the ball barehanded and throw, all in the same motion. The secret to this play is always to field the ball with your left foot forward. When you throw, always try to grip the ball across the seams. Your throw will be much more accurate and the ball will have a tendency to ride. When you're between the seams, the ball has a tendency to sail.

Always a problem for the third baseman is that he is blind so far as the sign to the pitcher from the catcher is concerned. The shortstop must tip him off if the pitcher is throwing a change-up or slow curve so he can adjust to the pitch.

Basically, I play third from a position about ten to fifteen feet behind the base and ten to twelve feet inside the foul line. That spot changes for each player according to his own ability to cover ground, how well he throws, and what the pitcher does—but, most important, who the batter is.

When Horace Clark of the Yankees, for example, is the batter, it's necessary to play in a little tighter because of his speed. When Maury Wills was with the Dodgers, there were two concerns—his great speed and a fantastic ability to bunt.

When some power hitter like Harmon Killebrew or Frank Howard is up there, you can play just about as deep as you want since they don't run real well. It was different with Mickey Mantle and Al Kaline back in the days when they were at the top of their ability. You didn't dare play deep on them. Not only did they have that pure power to drive a ball through you but they had the speed to leg out a chopper before you could throw them out.

I've often been asked what the most memorable play is that I've ever made. My immediate response is to talk about a couple of the drives I pulled down against the Reds in the 1970 World Series. Second thoughts always blot those out with another play that took place in 1968 or 1969. Frank Howard hit a line drive to me so hard it was just a blur. I jumped as high as I could, but the ball whizzed by overhead, so fast it actually made a wind current I could feel. Before I hit the ground Howard's drive had ricocheted off the left field wall and bounced about forty feet back onto the outfield grass.

I didn't think too much about it until I got back to the dugout. Then I broke into a cold sweat. If I had jumped quicker and higher, that ball might have hit me right in the face. And at the speed and power it was traveling, it would have torn my head off.

If there's one essential piece of advice I'd give to anyone trying to play third base, it is to get your glove down on the ground and in position to field the ball before you do anything else. Most balls that are booted for errors cause trouble because the glove is not down low enough to handle them. Get the glove on the dirt or the grass.

If the ball takes an erratic hop or jumps up at you, it's much easier and quicker to come up for the ball than to go down for it. Try to "see" the ball right into your glove— never take your eye off it. Many young players get into the habit of turning their head away from the ball as it gets near their glove. That's a natural fear reflex that must be overcome; it's those few inches from the glove where errors are made.

I learned another bitter lesson in 1966 during the hectic days of the American League race which we won and which put us into the World Series with the Dodgers. We were playing the Angels in Baltimore when a sharply hit grounder tore right through my glove. Some time before, the webbing in my glove had broken and I hadn't noticed it. That error cost us a run. Fortunately, Frank Robinson hit a homer later on to win the game for us.

Ever since, I have made a check of the webbing every day; in fact, usually just before I take the field each inning. If I notice the leather lacing starting to wear, I replace it. It's important to keep a close check on all your equipment from your shoes up.

One of the most difficult problems of playing third is chasing down pop flies. They can be unbelievably treacherous, especially if they get in the sun or in the middle of a battery of lights at night. As best I can remember, I've dropped very few. I remember dropping one against the Yankees in 1960 that gave them two or three runs, but it was on a day when they walloped us by a score of 16–0 or something equally embarrassing. I dropped one in Fort Lauderdale around 1965 or so during an exhibition and another, I remember, in 1969 in Boston right in front of our dugout.

Third base can be a hectic position. For example, I've read from time to time how many fellows have played third for the Dodgers since they moved to Los Angeles. That figure is up there in the forties somewhere.

Not too long ago, Doug Brown, who covers the Orioles for the *Baltimore Sun,* asked me if I knew how many men have played shortstop besides me in the years I've been with Baltimore. I really hadn't given it too much thought, but I was aware over all those years between 1955 when I played in six games and 1958 when I became a regular that there had been a lot of them.

Running down the list of those names seems almost like a TV replay of my whole baseball life for me: Jerry Adair, Luis Aparicio, Bobby Avila, Mark Belanger, Marv Breeding, Jim Brideweser, Chico Carrasquel, Foster Castleman,

[173]

Wayne Causey, Billy Cox, Jerry DaVanon, Chuck Diering, Chico Fernandez, Jim Finigan, Bob Floyd, Billy Gardner, Billy Goodman, Bob Grich, Ron Hansen, Woody Held, Billy Hunter, Bob Johnson, Dave Johnson, Billy Klaus, Fred Marsh, Eddie Miksis, Willie Miranda, Mickey McGuire, Buddy Peterson, Chico Salmon, and Bob Saverine.

In addition, Dick Williams and Don Leppert may have been in there part-time at shortstop. If they were, that would make a total of thirty-three players at that position during my years alone.

There are a lot of memories when you look over a list like that. I can never forget Bob Johnson, whom we called Rocky. He used to break us up with his antics. One day he flipped his sunglasses down going after an easy grounder. Another time, with one out and the tying run on third and the winning run on second, a pop-up came his way. Down came the glasses while Bob cradled the ball carefully in his glove, then casually rolled the ball toward the pitcher's mound. It was only the second out and the tying and winning runs both scored.

But hold on there—I forgot a shortstop. Me. I couldn't very well play beside myself at third but I did play four games or so at short. The last time Paul Richards moved me there for the eighth and ninth innings, I got all six put-outs—three pop-ups and three grounders. I haven't been back since.

Chapter 23

It takes a lot of people to make a ball club a contender and ultimately a champion. And I don't mean just the players, the coaches, and the managers. The effort has to start from the bat boy and move right up to the owner, Jerold Hoffberger, who's really chairman of the board of the Orioles. It includes all the girls in the office who keep the paper work rolling and all the scouts out in the boonies looking for young prospects like Brooks Robinson or Paul Blair or Boog Powell. The groundskeepers and the switchboard operators. Everyone.

No one has ever won anything alone, not even a game of marbles. That's what make the Orioles go. No doubt I'm prejudiced, but it is my feeling that the solid base on which we've been built over the years was created by Paul Richards. He put down a foundation that's never cracked. Hank

Bauer helped perpetuate it on the field and now Earl Weaver is keeping us all together and in contention year in and year out.

The manager's image has changed since Richards's tenure with the Orioles—especially in the major leagues. Now he has a lot of help around: coaches, trainers, scouts, and so on. The situation is not like that in the minors where a man like George Staller has to do everything from teaching a rookie how to put on a uniform to sweeping out the clubhouse. A major league manager just doesn't have the aura of respect around him that young players just coming up see in minor league managers.

There are too many veteran players around who are set in their ways. Some have been around longer than the manager. Perhaps we're pampered a bit. Perhaps some of us feel we know more about the game than the man running the show. On the few occasions I've had thoughts like that I have tried to keep them to myself.

I wouldn't want to be a major league manager. My friends can't understand that, it all looks so simple. It isn't.

The ideal manager is the man who is able to have the respect of everyone but can also get along with every player. Whatever the manager says goes, so far as I'm concerned. I may not agree. But I keep my mouth shut—most of the time—and fall into line.

Rarely have I gotten into a public debate with any of our managers in all my years in baseball.

But it has happened.

My biggest blowup was in 1972. It was early June and we were playing terrible ball—under .500. No one was hitting, and we had lost about five in a row when Earl told one of the writers that maybe some of the veterans—I felt he implied I was in that category—were over the hill.

For the first time in my life, I fired back publicly.

"I find the remark embarrassing," I told the press. "I don't enjoy going places to hear people say I'm over the hill, or know that they're thinking it."

Earl's rebuttal was that he had made those remarks to light a fire under us, to get us going, to break us out of our slump. Chan Keith, a baseball writer with the *Baltimore News-American,* had a long interview with me on the subject after I had made eight hits and driven in five runs in four games.

"I don't believe those hits have anything to do with Earl's remarks," I told Chan. "I don't feel he lit any fires under me. If a guy feels that way about something, I'd rather he spoke to me man-to-man. Not that Earl and I haven't had some talks lately, because we have. But for a comment like that to go on the national news wires—well, I didn't appreciate it.

"I know that Weaver has to worry for his job and I know he had to do something. He said what he thought he had to. That's a manager's prerogative. But that doesn't mean I like it."

But Earl Weaver is a great baseball manager. He's proven that. Rarely have I questioned his action, and that one incident is about the only time I ever did so publicly. Even after I said what I did, I wished I hadn't spouted off. I didn't really accomplish much except release a bit of my own anger.

Having to handle things like that gives me doubts about being a manager. I wouldn't worry about the decisions on the field—when to pull a pitcher, when to hit and run, when to bunt. It's the little things, the personal matters, that would get to me. And I'm sure it must get to Earl and every other manager in baseball.

Another factor that deters my interest in major league managing is the necessity for gaining minor league experience. Although there are those who have done without it, I really don't think there is any other way you can be qualified. But I just can't see going way back down and starting all over again to learn all the little things from a manager's viewpoint that you had to learn as a player.

When the time comes for me to give up my active career as a player, it's going to be a tough transition not to wake up each day and get mentally ready to play ball. The thought frightens me a little. I've never done anything else, nor wanted to, other than play ball. Whether or not there is going to be a big void when I'm finished I don't know, but there'll certainly have to be an adjustment of some kind.

Of all the adjustments that a pro athlete must make when he quits—the toughest will be not picking up that big pay check every two weeks. I've been fortunate through my career to see my salary climb up gradually from that first $4,000 a season to the $100,000 area.

The Lord has been kind to me. Few people earn that kind of money. Even fewer earn it doing what they like to do. It's a remarkable country that allows some of us to entertain folks and be paid such a great salary for doing what is really fun.

I feel I've worked hard at it, that I've given the very best that is in me every day. At the same time, I've tried to set an example for other players in the game and I hope that I have been successful. One of the nicest things ever said about me was Earl Weaver's observation the year I signed a $100,000 contract: "Brooks Robinson's the first man on the field, the first man on the bus." To me that remark meant that Earl Weaver considered me a team man first, last, and always, and that's what I've always tried to be.

I'm not much on the material things of life. We have a nice home with nice furnishings and good food. I don't buy a lot of clothes. I don't belong to a country club. I don't drive a Cadillac. With four kids you need a station wagon and that's usually the family car.

I'm not big on jewelry, although I guess you could say I'm a watch freak since I have eight or nine, but four or five of them have come to me as awards. I enjoy music and have a nice record collection of favorite country westerns but nothing big. I belong to a couple of book clubs and do quite a lot of reading, mostly in areas where I want to improve my knowledge. Books about the Civil War and about World War II especially appeal to me.

Most everything in life I do in moderation. That I'm not gung ho on anything is pretty well exemplified by my temper. I seldom lose it. Connie's often asked, "Brooks Robinson, don't you ever get mad?"

She's not really serious. I do get mad once in a while. Just the same, I don't think I'm hard to live around. Only the kids probably think Dad is tough on them from time to time. Even that's debatable.

I try to be kind to the world because the world has been extremely kind to me. Some major league players object to the interest of fans, especially the autograph seekers. I don't. Because of my schedule I may sometimes have to tell those asking for my autograph that I'll give them one later. But even with those kids for whom I've signed a hundred times over the year, I sign again.

Fans are great. Over the years, I've made friends with hundreds of them. One of the greatest Oriole fans happens to be the president of my fan club. Mary Lou La Martina started the Brooks Robinson Fan Club when I first appeared on the scene in Baltimore back in 1955. Since then we have become good friends and she seldom misses a game. When someone writes to me about joining the fan club, I just turn the letter over to her and she takes charge.

My general fan mail—and most of us players get hundreds of letters every year—I turn over to Gwen Phillips. She is a secretary in the Orioles' front office and handles all that type of mail, sending out rafts of autographed picture cards each year. That's the most frequently requested item.

There are times when baseball fans really overwhelm me. When there are twenty or thirty thousand or so at the park, I find myself thinking in wonderment: "All those people come here and pay to see us play."

I find it particularly surprising that our appeal as sports celebrities extends to people of all ages and all walks of life. The little old ladies especially are unbelievable. Letters I get from some of them who are seventy or eighty years old occasionally tick off statistics about my career that I'm not aware of myself.

Enthusiasm and support like that is what makes baseball such a great game and so meaningful to those of us whom God has given the ability to play it.

Talk about baseball is loaded with worn-out clichés and trite expressions. One of the most often heard is that "you never win without the talent." That's so true. But even with the talent, we all have a lot of help. Without those loyal spectators around the country who come out night after night to the ball parks to give us an inspiration we'd never make it. And when their devotion leads them to give a player his own special night there just aren't words to express the way he feels.

Brooks Robinson Night, held by the club and my fans at Baltimore's Memorial Stadium near the end of the 1964 season, will always remain one of the great moments of my life.

There were nearly forty thousand people present for our game with the California Angels that night, and Connie and the kids were almost as excited as I was. Before play started, they gave us all kinds of gifts: fifty shares of stock in the Orioles which I still have; a beautiful Buick station wagon; a gorgeous mink stole for Connie; and a tricycle or bicycle for each of the children, depending on their ability to ride; a large freezer for the house in Lutherville to which we had just moved.

Then J. A. W. Iglehart, one of the larger stockholders in the club at that time, came out with a nicely wrapped package for me. As I unwrapped it I thought it was making funny sounds. Inside were two live ducks, symbolic of my skill with a shotgun at Mr. Iglehart's farm.

Along with Billy Hunter and some other players, I used to go duck hunting there. The rule was to give each hunter ten shots with which to get two ducks. Always perfect, 0 for 10, I never got closer to any ducks than those two I received from Mr. Iglehart.

Brooks Robinson Night remains an all-time personal highlight in my life. I hope everyone who was responsible for even the smallest part of it knows how sincere my gratitude was when I made my little speech thanking everyone. I was equally sincere when I expressed the hope that one day soon we could bring the World Series to Baltimore.

But 1964 was still not to be our year. Although we were in the thick of things throughout the season we tailed off near the end and failed in our pennant efforts. Boog Powell's bat, lost to us those final thirty days or so when he broke his hand, might have made the difference. But as it was, New York won again. The White Sox were second and we were third, two games out of first.

Nevertheless, it was probably my greatest year in the majors. I ended up hitting .317, second in the American League only to Tony Oliva of the Twins. I led the league in runs batted in at 118, four more than Dick Stuart of Boston; was second in hits with 194 (considerably behind Oliva's 217); and third in doubles with 35. And I established my major league high for home runs at 28.

In contention both before and since, I was voted the Most Valuable Player in the American League that year, an honor one must truly appreciate when he looks over his rivals. There were a lot of contenders in 1964—Tony Oliva, Mickey Mantle, Harmon Killebrew, and Elston Howard, to name a few.

Back in 1960, I finished third in the balloting behind Roger Maris and Mickey Mantle. In 1965 I was third again, behind Zoilo Versailles. In 1966 two of us from Baltimore led in the balloting. Frank Robinson, who had a fantastic season as we went on to our first World Series win, beat me out. He is the only player in all the history of baseball who has won the MVP award in both leagues, having also received it in 1961 with Cincinnati. That was a remarkable achievement by Frank. It's a great honor to be named the MVP or even get in the top three in the voting.

Another honor which fills me with pride is having four times been voted the most valuable member of the Orioles —1960, 1962, 1964, and 1971. And I'm grateful, too, to the fans of Baltimore, who honored me back in 1969 by naming me the "all-time favorite from 1954 through 1972." That's a difficult decision since many of them have probably not seen all the players in Oriole history.

One of the experiences I treasure most came in 1966. True, that was our first World Series year and also the year I was selected as most valuable player in the All-Star game. But there was another honor bestowed upon me that's not chronicled in any of the record books.

The people of Little Rock proclaimed the week of October

24, 1966, as Brooks Robinson Week. It was a wonderful thing for the boy who'd grown up there with dreams of a baseball career to come home and be so well received by all the folks he'd known over the years—and a lot he didn't, too, like the mayor and the governor and many others.

Very, very high among the cherished awards that have come to me is the Gold Glove. That's given each year to the one man at each position who is regarded as the most proficient fielder. I've been mighty fortunate to have been awarded the Gold Glove every year since 1960.

The votes have been cast by various groups over the years. At first the voting alternated between the players one year and the managers and coaches the next. Now the awards are voted by the managers and coaches.

It's ironic that such a prestigious honor should be a problem. But the award is rather large, namely, a gold-plated glove modeled life-size from the player's own. Though I have most of mine, I have also given some away. Billy Hunter, who did so much to improve my fielding by constant work over the years, has one. Billy's probably hit me a million grounders in that time. My parents have one, and so does my brother—they're scattered all over.

Boog Powell keeps insisting that I'm going to have to cut him in on one. Boog has never won a Gold Glove as the best fielding first baseman in the league, and I feel that's an injustice.

"You're just lucky you've got me over here," Boog needles me all the time, "because you wouldn't be a Gold Glove guy unless I dug all those bad throws out of the dirt."

That's true. Boog is a tremendous first baseman. One thing that makes him so great in my book is his size. He's a big, big man and a marvelous target to throw at. There's no doubt, ever, in your mind where first base is when Boog's playing. You just throw at that human house. Get it anywhere near him and he'll grab it.

Perhaps that's why he's never won a Gold Glove. Because of his size he gets to a lot of balls that other first basemen could never reach. But we know his value, and in 1970 he was named the MVP of the American League.

A former all-state high school tackle on the same Key West team with George Mira, Boog was recruited by almost every college in the country. But Boog wanted to play baseball, and that's a good thing for the Orioles. Every time we make Boog dig one out of the dirt or leap high into the air to haul a wild peg down, he comes back to the dugout smiling.

"That's forty-six," he'll exclaim, or, "that's forty-seven."

What he means is that's the forty-sixth or the forty-seventh time—or whatever number he has logged—that he's dug a bad throw out of the dirt. He just wants to let us know that, while one of us may get the Gold Glove, Boog's a good fielder, too.

Another thing that makes Boog such a valuable first baseman is his enormous strength. No one has ever knocked Boog Powell down or knocked a ball out of his mitt. There'd be a better chance of knocking down Baltimore Memorial Stadium or taking out one of the Colts' defensive tackles. Any Oriole who's ever won a Gold Glove with Boog on first owes a great deal of credit to his skill with the glove.

Another wonderful year personally for me was 1970. I was voted the most valuable player in the 1970 World Series, and in January 1971 I was named the outstanding professional athlete of 1970. As part of the latter honor, I was presented with the annual Hickok Award, a large gold, diamond-and-jewel-studded belt.

A staggeringly extravagant creation valued at $10,000,

that belt created quite a problem from a tax standpoint. Following the appraisal, we took out the diamonds to make jewelry for Connie—there were 26 small ones and one large five-carat stone—but left the other stones in it, including the rubies. After replacing the diamonds with synthetic stones, we donated the belt to the Little Rock Boys Club, where it rests today along with one of my Gold Glove awards.

There were a lot of stories and interviews about my being selected to receive the Hickok award. One of them contained a comment I still value as one of the finest things anyone ever said about me. To this day I don't know who made it.

One of the Orioles told a writer: "This may sound corny, but Brooks is the nicest, sweetest guy in all baseball.

"Let me put it this way—if Mary Poppins played baseball, she'd have B. Robinson stenciled across the back of her uniform."

Chapter 25

Over the years a lot of writers and commentators have written and said marvelous things about a guy who calls third base his home. Two comments remain particularly striking in my memory.

"They say," wrote Jim Murray of the *Los Angeles Times* in his nationally syndicated column, "that when Brooks Robinson retires he's going to take third base with him."

Later on Jim paid me the supreme tribute. "In the future," he stated, "Brooks Robinson will be the standard every third baseman will be measured by."

That makes you shiver just a little bit when your name is Brooks Robinson and you still hear from the old-timers about Pie Traynor. To be categorized in that circle is something else.

But for every incident that sends you soaring off into

space, there's always a put-down that brings you abruptly crashing back to reality.

On a commercial flight to Milwaukee one time I was back toward the rear of the first-class section. I was really hungry, but time after time as the stewardess served the meals she passed me by. After the third or fourth time I saw her go by with a tray and give it to someone else, I stopped her.

"May I have dinner, miss?" I asked, trying not to sound impatient.

"Yes, after I've served the ball players," she said.

That's all. Nothing else. Talk about being deflated—the guys around me gave me trouble for the rest of the trip and several days afterward.

Baseball is difficult to get up for *every* day—day after day, week after week. I do my best. But when it's an All-Star game, the playoffs, or a World Series, the problem simply doesn't exist for me. I've never gone along with the talk some of the players hand out about preferring the three days off instead of taking part in the All-Star game.

Even Connie feels that way. "Of course I'd like for you to have three days off," she's told me a time or two over the years, "but I'd still rather have you go to the All-Star game."

I've been in over three thousand ball games in my life—maybe more than thirty-five hundred if I could recollect every game between the sandlots and the World Series—and every one of them has left me some kind of memory. One that sticks with me far too firmly is something I did very poorly when I wanted to do so well.

I had called my folks the night before we were going to be on the Monday night TV game against the Boston Red Sox.

"Tomorrow's our thirty-fifth anniversary," Mom reminded me. "We're having friends over for dinner to watch the game, so play well."

I was perfect. I went 0 for 5, struck out twice, booted a ground ball for an error, and dropped a pop-up. After the game I wrote Mom and told her not to do that to me any more. I couldn't stand the pressure.

Some other memories I'm not especially proud of either are the times I've been caught in triple plays—all four of them when Baltimore was at bat. The first came on June 2, 1958, against Washington when I lined a shot to Rocky Bridges, who grabbed it, stepped on third and then threw to second, where it was relayed to first to nail me. Another took place on September 2, 1964, at Robert F. Kennedy Stadium in Washington. A third came in Baltimore against the Red Sox on August 18, 1965, and the fourth was in the second game of a doubleheader on August 6, 1967, again with the Red Sox in Baltimore.

It's far more satisfying to remember the triple plays I initiated against our opponents. There have been three of those during my career in Baltimore. The first one was against Kansas City when Ellie Rodriguez laced one to me. I stepped on third to get one man and then threw to second for the out on the runner headed there. The second baseman's throw to first continued the whole play so smoothly it all looked easy.

In 1973 I started two triple plays. One was against Oakland when Gene Tenace hit a sharp liner to me at third. Instantly stepping on the bag, I went to second with my throw, and the relay to first got the runner there. Late in the season against Detroit, Frank Howard hit a ball to me with men on first and second, and we got a triple play exactly like the one that Tenace had hit into.

Now I don't know how many triple plays other players

have been in, but in my experience they are rare. In fact, the number of them I've been in up to now is the same as the number of World Series I've been in for Baltimore.

So far I agree with all those players who've told me that the first Series would stand out most sharply. Our first was in 1966. Having won the American League title with about ten days left in the season, we had quite a celebration in our clubhouse in Kansas City after the pennant-clinching game. During the party, Dick Hall, one of our relief pitchers, suggested that we make a team call to catcher Dick Brown, who was in Lake Worth, Florida, recovering from brain surgery. We used the phone in Hank Bauer's office, but the noise was hardly less deafening in there.

"Brownie," I remember yelling at him over the general pandemonium, "I hope you can hear me. This is the greatest. We've won it and we're thinking of you. You gave us a lot of hope and we hope you're coming along."

All the problems we had during that season were nothing compared to Dick Brown's, and we really did miss him.

That year the Dodgers didn't win the National League pennant until the final day of the season. Still, everyone favored them to win the series because of their great pitching. Sandy Koufax was a 27-game winner despite his arthritis, and in addition they had Don Drysdale, who'd won thirteen, and Claude Osteen, who'd won seventeen.

On the other hand, we'd lost Steve Barber for the season in mid-July. Wally Bunker had a sore arm and was a question mark. The only starters Hank Bauer could really count on were Jim Palmer and Dave McNally, plus whomever he could use from a bull pen of Hall, Stu Miller, Eddie Fisher, and Moe Drabowsky.

For the Dodgers this pennant was the thirteenth in their history. When we arrived in Los Angeles for a workout at

Dodger Stadium, some writer pointed out to Hank that the Dodgers had never lost a series since they'd been in Los Angeles. "We've never lost in Baltimore," snapped back that tough old one-time Marine gunner. He failed to add that this was our first series ever.

We got off to a great start, winning over Drysdale behind Dave McNally. We beat Don early. Frank Robinson, who'd won the triple crown that year, drove the ball into the seats in left field in the first inning. Drysdale's second pitch to me was a high fast ball, and I parked it in almost the same seats in the left field pavilion for back-to-back home runs.

We won that first one, 5–2, but then the next day found ourselves face to face with the impossible—Sandy Koufax. It wasn't a solid Sandy. He'd pitched twice in three days of the final week of the National League season. Though we knew his arm was hurting and tired, for four innings he was superb. But in the end, he couldn't stay with it, thanks to errors and some good hitting by all of us. It was Baltimore over Los Angeles, 6–0.

It was hard to believe we were two up as we flew East to resume the series. After our Wally Bunker, sore arm and all, went out and threw a six-hit, 1–0 shutout, we were in orbit —as was all of Baltimore. Then when McNally came back in the fourth game to pitch a four-hit, 1–0 shutout, I literally made a flying leap all the way from third base into Dave's arms. But I was the second one there. Our catcher, Andy Etchebarren, was ahead of me, shaking McNally's hand and pummeling him on the back all at the same time.

We didn't come down to earth for hours, though, as a matter of fact, our hitting was nothing to rejoice about. Even so, the Dodgers had lost to us in team batting with their .142. We are down in the record books for the worst batting average any team ever had in winning, 200. The fact that we still won and collected the winners' share has to reflect great credit on our pitching, something that supposedly belonged to the Dodgers.

The earned run averages proved how incredible it was. McNally was high with 1.59. Palmer, the best arm we had, had an 0.00, along with Bunker and Drabowsky. And he had won only fifteen games that whole year. Bunker, who had never pitched a shutout in his twenty-nine games of the season, proved what he could do when he pitched one in the series.

There's nothing in all of baseball more exhilarating than winning a World Series. You savor that all winter, living in another world that doesn't end even when you report to spring training.

There was a two-year lull between our first World Series and our second. In between, we had a managerial change that cost Hank Bauer his job midway in the 1968 season. Earl Weaver took over, and in 1969 we put together another pennant. But it didn't end in happiness as we lost the series to the New York Mets in five games.

Memorable moments for us were scarce in that series although Earl Weaver left his mark in history during the fourth game on October 15. With the Mets ahead at Shea Stadium in the third inning, plate umpire Shag Crawford decided he'd heard enough belly-aching from our side. So, marching over to our dugout, he instructed us in no uncertain terms to concentrate on our playing and leave the umpiring to him. As Crawford got back behind the plate, Earl strutted out to have his little say. That was all. Crawford gave Earl the hook. For only the third time in history, and the first time since 1935, a manager had been kicked out of a World Series game.

We weren't really in that series after the first game in Baltimore. Mike Cuellar's 4–1 win over Tom Seaver was even a little ironic in that it started with a home run by Don Buford. A football and baseball letterman at USC, Buford got that four-bagger off one of the Trojans' greatest pitching products—Seaver.

It was a long winter for all of us. But when 1970 was history, once again we were in the World Series, this time against an outstanding Cincinnati club. We took the series in five games, and it was the best short series I ever had in my life. It was so good, in fact, that I was voted the most valuable player.

The late Arthur Daley of the *New York Times* was one of the hundreds of writers who were most kind to me. In his column "Sports of the Times" he featured "The Brooks Robinson Story" as a follow-up to the series, and he included a summary of my play.

"First game—*Batting:* Hit a game-winning home run in the seventh for a 4–3 Oriole victory. *Fielding:* Robbed Lee May of a double with a spectacular backhander, cutting off a run because a single followed.

"Second game—*Batting:* Drove in the tying run and scored the winning run while setting off a five-run inning. *Fielding:* Again robbed May of a two-base hit and turned it into an inning-ending double play.

"Third game—*Batting:* Lashed out two doubles and started the scoring by driving in the first two runs. *Fielding:* Robbed Johnny Bench of a certain hit with a diving catch.

"Fourth game—*Batting:* He merely had a perfect day with four hits, including a homer. *Fielding:* The bum looked human. He handled only one routine chance.

"Fifth game—*Batting:* His single gave him a World

Series average of .429. *Fielding:* Made an impossible diving catch on Bench across the foul line in the ninth and started the last out of the series.

"The only thing that Robby didn't rob Bench of was the kid's sense of humor. When the Boy Wonder heard that the Orioles' 'Mr. Impossible' had won the sports car from *Sport* magazine as the outstanding World Series performer, the Redleg catching marvel offered a thought.

" 'The rumor is,' he said, 'that the car has an oversized glove compartment.' "

We were able to make it to the World Series the third time in succession in 1971, and I hope I proved my worth in helping get us there. But Pittsburgh took us right down to seven games before they won, 2–1, to earn one of those big championship rings.

One of the nice mementoes of our showing in that World Series came to me from Rawlings, the sporting goods manufacturer for whom I have endorsed a Brooks Robinson glove throughout my career. Royalties from sales have been substantial over the years, and in 1970 Harry Figge, Jr., chairman of A.T.O., of which Rawlings is a subsidiary, presented me with 975 shares of the company's stock—a number matching my composite fielding average for the previous ten years. It was a nice gift to receive since the market value was about $10,000 at the time.

An ultimate and tangible fringe reward every player aspires to is the share voted to players for participating in championship and World Series play-offs. In four of those great affairs the Orioles have received—per man—sums of not quite $12,000 to more than $18,000.

But the most important rewards of a career are not the financial ones or even the marks in the record books. They are the feelings you have about what you are doing—the happiness of being able to give yourself to a job you love, the sense of worth for being able to give others something to enjoy, the sense of accomplishment that comes from giving your best efforts.

From my earliest years, my obsession with baseball and the goal of becoming a major league player was well known not only to my family and my coaches but to most of my teachers. I can never thank them enough for their interest and understanding—even their attempts to convince me to go a different direction from the one I chose. Maybe I would have been successful in another field.

But there's one thing I'm sure of. In baseball and at third base I found a home that surpasses the grandest castle anyone could ever dream of building.

Acknowledgments

To my wife, who aided me so diligently in reconstructing many events from the past, go my special thanks. And to Jack Tobin, who worked tirelessly in turning our hours of interview into this narrative, special expressions of gratitude are due.

We are also grateful for the assistance of Bob Brown, public relations director of the Orioles, in gathering statistical material; to Mrs. Gaye Gilpin, who transcribed the miles of interview tapes; and especially to our editors, Floyd Thatcher, vice president and executive editor of Word Books, and Mrs. Pat Wienandt, who guided the entire project from manuscript to published form.

Information in this Appendix is reproduced from Baltimore Orioles club brochure, through courtesy of Robert W. Brown, Public Relations Director of the Orioles

Appendix

BROOKS ROBINSON

Born: May 18, '37; 6'1"; 190; Bats, R; Throws, R.

Year	Club	Pct.	G	AB	R	H	2B	3B	HR	RBI	SB	CS	HP	BB	SO
1955	York*	.331	95	354	72	117	17	3	11	67	1	..	6	47	64
1955	Baltimore	.091	6	22	0	2	0	0	0	1	0	0	0	0	10
1956	San Antonio	.272	154	577	72	157	28	6	9	74	1	2	4	54	57
1956	Baltimore	.227	15	44	5	10	4	0	1	1	0	0	0	1	5
1957	Baltimore	.239	50	117	13	28	6	1	2	14	1	0	1	7	10
1957	San Antonio	.266	33	124	10	33	5	1	1	9	0	1	0	5	16
1958	Baltimore	.238	145	463	31	110	16	3	3	32	1	2	5	31	51
1959	Baltimore	.284	88	313	29	89	15	2	4	24	2	2	2	17	37
1959	Vancouver	.331	42	163	20	54	9	2	6	30	2	1	0	6	14
1960	Baltimore	.294	152	595	74	175	27	9	14	88	2	2	0	35	49
1961	Baltimore	.287	163	668	89	192	38	7	7	61	1	3	4	47	57
1962	Baltimore	.303	162	634	77	192	29	9	23	86	3	1	1	42	70
1963	Baltimore	.251	161	589	67	148	26	4	11	67	2	3	1	46	84
1964	Baltimore	.317	163	612	82	194	35	3	28	118	1	0	4	51	64
1965	Baltimore	.297	144	559	81	166	25	2	18	80	3	0	2	47	47
1966	Baltimore	.269	157	620	91	167	35	2	23	100	2	3	5	56	36
1967	Baltimore	.269	158	610	88	164	25	5	22	77	1	3	4	54	54
1968	Baltimore	.253	162	608	65	154	36	6	17	75	1	1	4	44	55
1969	Baltimore	.234	156	598	73	140	21	3	23	84	2	1	3	56	55
1970	Baltimore	.276	158	608	84	168	31	4	18	94	1	1	4	53	53
1971	Baltimore	.272	156	589	67	160	21	1	20	92	0	0	3	63	50
1972	Baltimore	.250	153	556	48	139	23	2	8	64	1	0	2	43	45
1973	Baltimore	.257	155	549	53	141	17	2	9	72	2	0	3	55	50
Major League Totals		.271	9354		1117	2539	430	65	251	1230	26	23	48	748	881
			2504												

* Signed by Baltimore as free agent on 6/1/55.

Honors: "Most Valuable Player," 1970 World Series . . . "Most Valuable Player," 1966 Major League all star game . . . American League "Most Valuable Player," 1964 . . . Finished second in American League "MVP" balloting in 1966 and third twice (1960 and 1965) . . . "Most Valuable Oriole" four times (1960–62–64–71) . . . Named to the American League all star team by *The Sporting News* nine times (1961–62–64–65–66–67–68–71–72) . . . Selected all time favorite Oriole in fan vote, 1969 . . . Won Hickok Belt in January, 1971 . . . Named to every American League all star team since 1960 and has played in 17 straight games . . . Winner of "Gold Glove" award as best defensive third baseman in every year since 1960 (14 straight) . . . Honored by Advertising Club of Baltimore as city's "Man of the Decade," January, 1972 . . . Recipient of Commissioner's Trophy in February, 1972, as player "who best typifies the game of baseball both on and off the field" . . . Was chosen from among three other finalists (Kaline, Killebrew, Banks) . . . Willie Mays was only previous winner.

Fielding: Holds following major league records for third basemen—most games, career (2,488); most assists, career (5,315); most chances accepted (excluding errors), (7,736); most double plays, career (531); highest fielding average, career, 1,000 or more games, .971 (230 errors in 7,966 chances); most years leading third baseman in fielding average (10) . . . Holds following American League records for third basemen—most games, season, 163 (1961, 1964); most years leading in games, 8; most years leading in assists, 7 . . . Winner of 14 straight "Gold Glove" awards (1960–73) . . . Amazed everyone when he committed three errors in one inning (6th) in a game against Oakland 7/28/71, the night after he had played hero's role by blasting a two-run homer with two out in 9th to win game off Rollie Fingers. The night of the three errors, Frank Robby came to his rescue with a three-run game winning shot in the 9th, also off Rollie Fingers.

All-Star play: Has .310 batting average (13–for–42) while appearing in 17 straight all star games dating back to 1960 . . .

Selected "Most Valuable Player" in 1966 at St. Louis when he had three hits, including a triple, while handling eight chances in the field . . . Homered in 1967 game . . . Hits include three triples . . . Has handled 43 total chances in field without committing an error . . . Leading A.L. vote-getter in 1971 fan balloting (1,110,469).

World Series play: Among leading hitters in 1971 World Series . . . Batted .318 (7-for-22) and paced O's with five runs batted in . . . Performance in 1970 Series vs. Cincinnati ranks among greatest ever by an individual . . . Selected "Most Valuable Player" . . . Tied record for most hits in five-game series while batting .429 with 9-for-21 . . . Hits included two doubles and two home runs and he drove in six runs . . . Had four hits in fourth game . . . Charged with error on first fielding play but was brilliant after that . . . Batted only .053 (1-for-19) in 1969 Series vs. Mets . . . Had 3-for-14 (.214) in 1966 Series vs. Dodgers, including a home run in 1st inning of 1st game . . . Has made only three errors in 75 total chances.

Career: Most hits by a third baseman in baseball history, 2,539. Has been with O's all or part of last 19 seasons . . . Led A.L. with 118 rbi in '64 . . . Has .404 average (23-for-57) in four championship series covering fourteen games . . . Batted .500 (7-for-14) in '69 and .583 (7-for-12) in '70 (both against the Twins) then hit .364 (4-for-11) vs. Oakland in the '71 ALCS.

Has hit six grand slams in his career: 7/31/60 vs. Cleveland (Gary Bell) at Balto.; 5/6/62 at California—Dodger Stadium (Ken McBride); 5/9/62 (very next game) vs. K.C. A's (Ed Rakow) at Balto.; 7/70 vs. N.Y. (Lindy McDaniel) at Balto.; 7/18/71 at Oakland (John Odom), and 9/16/71 vs. N.Y. (Roger Hambright) at Balto.

Beaned by Woody Fryman in Detroit on 9/12/72 in 9th inning but came back to start next day . . . It was seventh time he had been hit in the head by pitched ball starting with Earl Wilson ('55), Ned Garver ('57), John Buzhardt ('63), Phil Niekro ('67), Steve Blass ('68), and Mike Nagy ('70).

Twice in career has put together strings of eight consecutive

hits: 7/10 through 7/15/60 and 8/21 through 8/23/63 . . .
Brooks has missed only 48 of the O's last 2,323 games ('60
through '73) . . . Four times he has played in every game, and,
in 10 of his big league seasons, he has missed three or fewer
. . . The only time he has been out of the lineup for any length
of time was in '65 when he missed 18 games because of a frac-
tured thumb (from a pitch by Hank Aguirre) and a shoulder
injury.

Personal: Orioles player representative . . . Visited U.S. military bases in Germany after '72 season . . . Retains interest in
sporting goods store which bears his name in Lutherville and
Gorsuch House Restaurant near Memorial Stadium . . . Orig-
inally signed by Arthur Ehlers . . . He and his wife, Connie,
were married in '60 and are the parents of four children: Brooks
David (7/24/61), Chris (2/22/63), Michael (3/11/64), and
Diana (2/22/68).